JOHN CHAMBERS AND THE CISCO WAY:

NAVIGATING THROUGH VOLATILITY

JOHN K. WATERS

JOHN CHAMBERS AND THE CISCO WAY:

NAVIGATING THROUGH VOLATILITY

JOHN WILEY & SONS, INC.

This book is printed on acid-free paper. ♾

Published simultaneously in Canada.

ISBN 0-471-00833-8

Printed in the United States of America.

10 9 8 7 6 5 4 3 2 1

DEDICATION

This book is dedicated to Beverly and Leo Waters, dyed-in-the-wool Midwesterners who hated to see their son move to California, but eventually got used to the idea.

ACKNOWLEDGMENTS

Every writer faces the blank screen alone, but no one creates a book single-handedly. Without the hard work, generous cooperation, and unflagging support of many others, this one simply would not have been possible. I'd like to thank everyone who helped me in this enterprise, but especially:

- Jeanne Glasser, acquisitions editor at John Wiley, who approved the project, supported it when the economic downturn put the future of Chambers and Cisco in doubt, and just generally tolerated my eccentricities throughout the writing and editing of this book.
- My agent, Margot Maley-Hutchison, for sticking up for me during the resolution of the inevitable differences that arise between author and publisher, and for some much-needed handholding.
- Production editor Kim A. Nir, for her professionalism and good humor; copy editor Pauline Piekarz, for her keen eye; marketing manager Elke Villa and her staff, for getting the word out; and designer Loretta Leiva, for getting all the words to look so good.

- All the folks at Graphic Composition, Inc. for getting this book typeset in record time.
- Author-journalist Sally Richards, a friend and colleague without whom I would never have undertaken this project.
- Writer-editor Paula Munier, for the book's original title. (Sorry we couldn't use it.)
- And Bay Area attorney Teresa M. Derichsweiler, for her tech-industry savvy, sophisticated literary sensibilities, and steadfast support. I couldn't have done it without you.

I am also deeply indebted to the many people who took the time to talk with me about their experiences with Mr. Chambers and Cisco Systems. I am particularly grateful to author and analyst Glenn Rifkin for his insights into Cisco's acquisitions strategies, and his anecdotes about the people who built the company; to analyst Ken Presti, for his historical perspectives on the networking industry, the company, and the economic downturn; and to Lorene "Kitty" Anderson-Walter, for her thoughtful recollections of Chambers's childhood struggles with dyslexia.

To those who chose to speak with me off the record, I wish I could give you the credit you deserve for your absolutely invaluable contributions to this book. In lieu of public acknowledgments, let me say, many, many thanks.

John K. Waters
December 2001

CONTENTS

JOHN CHAMBERS AND THE CISCO WAY:

NAVIGATING THROUGH VOLATILITY

INTRODUCTION: THE QUINTESSENTIAL INFORMATION AGE CEO

It is the spring of 2001, and Cisco Systems CEO John T. Chambers is speaking at a business luncheon in a hotel in Santa Clara, California, not far from the company's headquarters. He's dressed in a conservative business suit—his trademark—and, as always, he's talking fast, but softly, and with a southern courtliness that belies his position as chief executive of an industry-dominating high-tech company. He fixes his audience with his blue eyes, brushes a wispy lock of blond hair from his broad forehead, and you can hear the hills of West Virginia in his voice.

He is addressing a business-savvy local crowd, and they don't hesitate to ask about the implications of his company's recent reversals of fortune, about the efficacy of Cisco's vaunted acquisitions strategy and legendary virtual close in the light of those reversals, and about the future of the so-called New Economy, of which Chambers has been such a vocal, center-stage advocate. He answers their questions with characteristic optimism and a disarming forthrightness. He is there to calm worries about the economic downturn that has ravaged his industry, and to manage expectations about his company. He would be doing both of those things, in one way or another, all summer.

The tech wreck that had started as an e-commerce shakeout with the bursting of the dot com bubble, and had grown into a full-fledged economic downturn in 2001 that would eventually touch companies of virtually every size and stripe, had finally found its way to Cisco City. In March 2001, Cisco joined the burgeoning ranks of technology companies announcing layoffs and write-offs and earnings shortfalls.

Until that fateful spring, Cisco Systems had been a company that could do no wrong, and John Chambers was Wall Street's golden boy. From 1995, the year Chambers took over as CEO, to 2000, Cisco's revenues grew by an average annual rate of 57 percent. In March 2000, Cisco's market cap reached just over half a trillion dollars, and it was, for a shining moment, the most valuable company on earth. It didn't matter that it dropped quickly back into third place; everybody was still getting rich. From its initial public offering in 1990 to the spring of 2000, Cisco's share price grew by more than 94,000 percent, making millionaires of many of its investors, its executives, and even its rank-and-file employees.

Cisco continued to fly as high as ever for months after "burst" and "bubble" first began appearing in print and on Lou Dobbs' teleprompter. But it couldn't escape the black-hole gravitational pull of the downturn. In March, the company announced its first layoffs; two months later, it announced its first-ever losses.

And all of a sudden the book I was writing about John Chambers seemed to be a much more challenging project than I had thought it was going to be when I first took pen in hand a few months earlier. What began as an examination of the man behind the meteoric rise of a high-tech company had *evolved* rather abruptly, and I found myself writing a very different book.

Or so I thought then.

Throughout the summer of 2001, I watched as one of the most significant chapters in Chambers's professional life and in the history of his company unfolded before my eyes. The mettle of the man was tested in ways it had not been in a decade. That summer, virtually every one of the very strategies that had brought Cisco such phenomenal success was called into question. Only a few months earlier, business journalists were fawning over him, analysts were extolling the virtues of his management approach, and he was the investors' best friend. He was "Mr.

Internet," "The Best Boss in America," and "CEO of the Year" in about half a dozen business magazines. Now, they were taking potshots at him. Some critics were almost gleeful in their denunciation of Chambers's leadership. "Investors give new meaning to the phrase 'torture Chambers,'" *Fortune* quipped. "Cisco or Crisco?" wondered a *Business 2.0* headline.

In the decade-plus that I've been covering Silicon Valley for various computer and high-tech trade magazines, I had seen this kind of knee-jerk reaction before. An industry analyst once described the phenomenon to me this way: "The high-tech sector regularly kills its own visionaries; yesterday's genius is today's dogmeat."

Cisco was hardly alone on the downward slope. In Silicon Valley, were I live and work, Internet companies were closing down in droves and high-tech operations were handing out pink slips by the bucketful. Hosts of name-brand companies like Hewlett-Packard, Intel, and Sun Microsystems announced layoffs and lowered expectations. Even Cisco's chief rival in the optical-networking market, Juniper Networks, was cutting its workforce and profit projections. In the summer of 2001, anyone looking to rent a moving van in the Valley would have been hard pressed to find one.

And yet Chambers seemed to be taking most of the heat that summer. He had been at Cisco's helm for one of the fastest and loftiest ascents in high-tech history, and for one of the industry's steepest and deepest plunges. The company was unique in that regard, and so it was probably inevitable that Chambers would take the lion's share of the flack. (And he had made such an *issue* of his desire to avoid those layoffs.)

But the truth is, he probably didn't deserve it. As summer turned into fall, despite the downturn and the braying of the naysayers, Cisco Systems remained one of the most powerful and important organizations in the tech sector. As I write these words, rumors that Cisco might acquire a Sunnyvale, California-based networking firm have caused that company's stock to rise sharply for the third straight day. Being acquired by Cisco may not be the IPO-like exit strategy today that it was a year ago, but the very idea still sets more than a few hearts a-thumping.

And John Chambers continues to be one of the most compelling CEOs in America. In Silicon Valley, where you can't swing a dead cat without hitting a remarkable chief executive, that's saying something.

I first wrote about Cisco back in 1991, when I profiled the company—along with ninety others—for a book called *Silicon Valley: Inventing the Future* (with Jean Deitz Sexton, Windsor Publications, 1992). The company had gone public a year earlier, "Cisco" was still spelled with a lowercase C, and its colorful founders had only recently moved on to greener pastures. John Chambers joined the company in January of that year, but I wasn't paying much attention to sales execs. For reasons I never learned, that Cisco profile didn't make it into the book, but my interest in the company was well and truly piqued.

Over the years, I've watched the company grow and change, and I've watched its CEO emerge as a leading light in high tech. Chambers was and is a chief executive who *gets it.* He's not enamored of the technology he sells for its own sake; to him, it's a tool and a commodity. In an environment in which competing technologies can ignite what amount to religious wars, Chambers's agnosticism is refreshing.

And so is his optimism, which he uses not to hide from unpleasant realities or to pump sunshine for his company's investors but to push himself to reach beyond his grasp. Even Chambers's most buoyant statements are surprisingly grounded. During the question-and-answer period that followed the speech mentioned at the beginning of this introduction, I asked Chambers whether he would have done anything differently had he known what he knew then six months earlier. Without missing a beat, he said, "Of course." And he quickly added, "But that question isn't really very useful. A better question might be, what did you learn from the experience? We learned that change can occur at a much more rapid magnitude than we ever thought possible, and we will position ourselves better on that in the future. Will we stop taking calculated business risks? Absolutely not!"

This book focuses on John Chambers the CEO, but it's also a chronicle of his life, from his childhood struggles to overcome a learning disability to lessons learned during his professional formative years, and finally to his role in the evolution of an industry. It is, I hope, a fair portrait of a hard-working and astonishingly successful executive facing some of the greatest challenges of his career.

My research for this project included interviews with current and former employees, contractors, customers, industry analysts, competitors, old friends, and teachers. Many of these people asked not to be identified, and I have respected their requests for anonymity in these pages. Among those who know John Chambers, I found a genuine fondness and deep respect for the man—even among those who were laid off. One former employee told me that Chambers was a "phenomenal human being." Another said that he was the "coolest guy." One executive came close to cracking nasty about Chambers when he told me that his "nice-guy image" is a bit of smoke and mirrors. "It's a cultivated persona," he said. "The guy isn't Mr. Rogers." But even that remark was a left-handed compliment; the ability to play hardball isn't necessarily a bad quality in a CEO. Others insisted that he is, in fact, very much like the cardigan-wearing PBS kiddie-show host—on steroids maybe, a Type A Mr. Rogers perhaps, but nice.

I don't know if you can call John Chambers the best CEO in America, but he certainly must be included on any list of America's top chief executives. He's not as well known to the public as many of his peers, but he is as influential as anyone in business today, and he just may be the quintessential Information Age CEO.

CHAPTER 1

A WEST VIRGINIAN CHOIRBOY

On November 30, 1994, a small headline appeared on the business page of *The Charleston Gazette.* It read: "City Native Chosen to Head California Computer Firm." In the brief article that followed, residents of West Virginia's capital city learned that 45-year-old John T. Chambers had been named president and CEO of "a California-based Fortune 500 computer firm." A local boy who had already made good had just made even better.

This wasn't the first time John Chambers' name had appeared in his hometown newspaper. In 1988, the *Gazette*'s "Business Briefs" section carried the announcement of Chambers' promotion to senior vice president at Wang Laboratories, another "Fortune 500 computer company." It ran just above the announcement that Gardner's Gentle-Care Drycleaning and Laundry had returned to downtown Charleston with the opening of a new store in the Pritchard Building.

By the time the first year of the new millennium had drawn to a close, Chambers was rating banner headlines in the hometown paper. In its New Year's Eve 2000 edition, the *Gazette* shouted: "Cisco CEO John Chambers 2000 West Virginian of The Year, State Native Architect Behind One of World's Largest Firms."

Chambers was the city's best and brightest, a symbol of success, and a product of the area's values. He wasn't just a hometown boy who had made good; he was—and is—a local hero.

KANAWHA CITY

John Thomas Chambers wasn't much of a headline grabber in the years before he sat down in the CEO's chair at Cisco Systems. He was born in Cleveland, Ohio, on August 23, 1949, but his family moved to Charleston, West Virginia, soon after his birth.

Charleston was a small city—still is, with a population of just over 57,000. It grew up along the banks of the Elk and Great Kanawha rivers, where the two waterways flowed together, not far from the Appalachian Mountains. Chambers and his two younger sisters grew up in Kanawha City (pronounced *k'NAH-wuh* locally), a flat stretch of developed land and foothills just across the big river from downtown Charleston.

Chambers grew up in an educated, solidly middle class household. Both of John's parents were doctors; one grandfather was a bank president, and the other ran a construction company. A childhood friend once characterized his family life as "all Donna Reed and Leave It to Beaver."[1]

John Turner "Jack" Chambers was a prominent obstetrician/gynecologist with an interest in real-estate development and health-care ventures. During his years in medical practice, Jack Chambers delivered about six thousand babies, including all four of West Virginia Senator Jay Rockefeller's children. He also once ran unsuccessfully for the state senate as a Republican.

June Chambers worked as an internist and psychiatrist. She was known as a conscientious mother who brought hot glazed doughnuts home to John and his sisters after school. Chambers has often given credit to his mother—a warm, friendly, and insightful woman— for his people skills. His interest in business came from his father, and perhaps his talent for it, too. Chambers has talked about his father's ability to spot important trends, to see where things were headed. He often tells the story of how, in the 1970s, Jack Chambers foresaw the coming consolidation in health care before most of his colleagues, and how he led the merger of nine small hospitals in Charleston, even through the opposition of their boards.

The people in his hometown remember the young John Chambers as a personable, cheerful, and very smart boy. Old friends say that he was focused and hardworking, a team player, and a kid who didn't believe in taking shortcuts. Teachers remember him as an excellent student, very disciplined and respectful of his elders, and something of a parent pleaser.

And he was competitive. Very competitive.

"John played a lot of sports, but he was never the star," Jack Chambers recalled in a 1998 interview. "He liked to organize teams and always expected them to win. He wouldn't have played if he didn't."[2]

John played in church-league basketball and in Little League, and he participated in the Cub Scouts. Bill Nottingham, owner of the Charleston Bicycle Center in Kanawha City and a childhood friend of Chambers, remembers him as a nice guy but very competitive when it came to sports. "We were always good friends," he said in an interview, "but on the basketball court he would do anything to beat me." Jim Buckalew, a former athletic director at the University of Charleston who now works for the U.S. Rowing Association and who roomed with Chambers at West Virginia University, remembers John as a tough competitor who never forgot a defeat. "He did not like to lose," he said.[3]

Chambers is still a basketball fan, and he reportedly still keeps in touch with his childhood pals. Nottingham told the *Charleston Gazette* in 1999 that he received a phone call from his old friend consoling him on the death of his mother. "One of the things in his success—his personal life has changed, but it really hasn't altered his personality," Nottingham said.[4]

Hunting and fishing with his father and his uncle Thomas Chambers, who owned camps on the Elk River, also played an important part in Chambers's life. John and his friends would visit the camps to hunt, fish, search for frogs, and go on "float trips" down the river that would sometimes last for days. In an article he wrote for the *New York Times* in May 2001, Chambers recounted two near-disaster fishing stories that profoundly influenced him:

> I got into trouble at 7. I was fishing in fast water where the bass feed. I went too far out on a rock. The current caught me, pulling me into the middle of the rapids. I was a good swimmer but not that good. I looked at Dad. He said, "Hold onto the fishing pole." I went down the rapids and Dad came and got me. I focused on the pole and felt unconditional trust and confidence.
>
> Five years later, in the same river, a metal pipe hit me in the head. Blood gushed. I started running toward the house a half-mile away. Mom didn't bat an eye. She put her hand on it and said: "It's a puncture wound; it probably won't require any stitches. You're going to be fine."[5]

From the first incident, he said, he learned the value of trust in others and focusing on the problem at hand; from the second, he learned the effectiveness of remaining calm in a crisis.

Chambers has continued to take his fishing seriously. Colleagues told me about the time, while on an executive retreat in Alaska, Chambers was so determined to catch the most fish that he kept one of his vice presidents out in a small boat for hours after a rainstorm had sent everyone else back to the lodge.

He would continue to find time every year to take weeklong fishing trips with his father. They would travel to Alaska, Key West, the Yucatán, and the Canadian Arctic. The two have remained especially close, and Chambers has often said that his father is a role model, a confidant, and his best friend. Forty years later, the father-and-son fishing trips include Chambers's own, now-grown son, John Jr.

DYSLEXIA, DOUBT, AND DETERMINATION

Both of Chambers's parents, not surprisingly, put a high priority on education, and even as a young boy, their son tried his best to measure up to their expectations. But by the time John had reached the age of eight, it was clear that something was wrong. He was having trouble learning to read. At the blackboard, the teacher was writing W-A-S, but John was seeing S-A-W.

His old friends say that John managed to hide his dyslexia from all but the closest of his friends. A former classmate recalls that his problem was not readily apparent to his peers, and that it didn't seem to slow him down in school. But, of course, he was struggling, and other accounts hold that John's young classmates made fun of him.

Chambers has said that he considered his dyslexia a weakness, and never talked about it as a youngster. He felt dumb, and he couldn't understand why he was falling behind in school. And then the teachers began to treat him differently—at least that's how it seemed to John. In their eyes he saw something he never saw in his parents' eyes: doubt. It seemed as though they weren't sure he was going to make it through high school, let alone go on to college.

Jack and June Chambers, however, had no doubts about their only son. Maybe, as his father would later recall, "John thought he wasn't as smart as the other kids,"[6] but his mother and father knew better. Whatever the trouble was, they were not going to sit back and watch their son fall behind in school.

Lorene Anderson-Walter—then Kitty Anderson—was a reading specialist for state and county schools. She had a national reputation, wrote textbooks, journal articles, and newsletters, and lectured widely. Her private reading clinic attracted a wide range of clients, from struggling students to adult professionals. June Chambers sought her out and brought young John to her for testing.

"He was completely failing in reading," Anderson-Walter told me. "He thought his teacher had said that he would never learn to read. I don't think that was true. The teacher may have said that he would have a hard time. Back then, very few people knew anything about dyslexia. It was almost a disgrace to have it."

Anderson-Walter tested John and confirmed that his problem was dyslexia. She could tell immediately that the boy was "extremely bright." (Dyslexics often are.) She explained to John's mother that it would take some time and tutoring, and although it couldn't be done overnight, she could teach Johnny to read. Anderson-Walter remembers that despite the strong stigma attached to dyslexia, June Chambers was unusually calm as she received the news that her son had a learning disorder.

"She was very interested and seemed to understand what I was saying," Anderson-Walter says, "and she wasn't panic stricken by the word 'dyslexia.' I tried very hard to stay away from that word at that time, because of the stigma. I could not believe that a mother would be so interested in every detail, the way she was. Naturally, I'm for this, so I told her more than she needed to know. I even got out charts to show her. Of course, I didn't realize that she was a medical doctor."

John would visit Kitty twice a week for two hours for about a year and a half. "I don't remember ever having a more determined student," she says. "There was just no doubt in his mind that he was going to learn to read. He came in smiling, and he had these great big eyes. And he was anxious to get to work. He would take any assignment I gave him. Nothing was too small. Some of the things we did back then probably seemed very babyish to him, things like underlining every word. But you're trying to get them to read left to right, you see. He was perfectly willing to do anything of that sort."

The press has often described Chambers's learning disability as a "mild form of dyslexia." Anderson-Walter disagrees with that characterization: "It wasn't the worst case I've every seen, but it wasn't *mild*. What made the difference was John himself. He was a very, very bright boy, and *so* determined. If he hadn't been, it would have taken much longer."

That John Chambers had to overcome dyslexia as a child is no secret today, but it wasn't always so widely known. In 1995, Cisco employees would learn about it during a "bring-your-kid-to-work" event, when a little girl who was trying to speak to an assembled group couldn't get her question out and started to cry. "I have a learning disability," she said, whereupon Cisco's newly appointed CEO jumped up to comfort her. "So do I," he told her—and hundreds of his employees. "Take your time."

In his *New York Times* piece, Chambers wrote about the aftermath of his impulsive revelation:

> I was a little bit embarrassed. That evening, there were a dozen e-mail messages. One said, "You don't know what it meant for my child." Parents and children encouraged me to be more candid with my learning disability, how I overcame it and share with young people not to use a learning disability as an excuse for why we can't do things in life.[7]

"The thing I remember most about John Chambers," says Anderson-Walter "was his constant smiling. He had this very optimistic attitude about everything. About his whole life. About everything he did. He was just not going to fail. One thing I notice as I hear him now on TV is that he still has that attitude."

Despite his dyslexia—or perhaps because of it—John would graduate second in his class as Charleston High School's 1967 salutatorian. He went on to earn three college degrees, but he never learned to like reading, and he avoids it whenever possible. As CEO of Cisco Systems, he instructs his employees to boil reports down to summaries. Famous for a powerful memory that allows him to recall nearly everything he has heard in meetings, he usually gives speeches and presentations without notes. He prefers voice mail to e-mail.

TWO LOVES: ELAINE AND EDUCATION

In high school, John and his friend Jim Buckalew used to double date. Chambers would drive on Friday night, and Buckalew would drive on

Saturday night. They usually took their dates to the movies or to the local miniature golf course. "There wasn't a lot to do back then," Buckalew said in an interview.[8]

Dull as the nightlife of 1960s Charleston may have been for the two teenagers, without it Chambers might never have met his future wife. According to Chambers, it was Buckalew's then-girlfriend who brought the two together. She had already fixed him up with two girls, but no sparks were flying. Out of desperation, she turned to her friend Elaine Prater. "She couldn't find the girl she was initially after," Chambers recalled later in an interview, "but found my wife. She told her, 'Elaine, I need a big favor.'"[9]

Buckalew remembers events slightly differently: "We were over at Stonewall [Jackson High School] on senior week and Elaine poked her head around the corner. John caught her eye and that was it." Buckalew then asked his girlfriend to arrange a meeting.[10]

However they got together, sparks did fly between John and Elaine. He took her to the prom, and they dated off and on for several years. After graduation, John enrolled at Duke University, but after only two years at Duke, he transferred to West Virginia University to be with Elaine, who was there studying to become a speech therapist. (Chambers has often joked that even his wife couldn't rid him of his West Virginia accent.)

Later, while John was studying for his graduate degree at Indiana University, he and Elaine finally tied the knot. Jack Chambers stood beside his son as his best man. After a reception at Edgewood Country Club, John and Elaine went to Las Vegas for their honeymoon. Many years later, Chambers would tell an interviewer that Elaine was the only person, outside his immediate family, whom he had ever told that he loved. "The longer we're married," Chambers said, "the closer we get."[11]

Although early in life he had expected to follow his parents' footsteps into medical school, in college John found himself following a different path. As a boy, he had worked in a motel and restaurant that his father owned, and that experience started him thinking about running his own company. He studied business as an undergraduate, detoured to take a law degree, but ended up studying business again on the graduate level.

When he transferred to WVU, Chambers shared an apartment with another old schoolmate, Joe Rice, now a Charleston dentist. Both were serious students: Rice was pre-med, and Chambers was pre-law. According to Rice, Chambers was a good student who studied hard but played hard, too—and knew how to separate the two. "We were both focusing in on what we wanted to do," he recalled later in an interview. "He took things as they came, but he also had his ducks in a row. A lot of people didn't do that."[12]

When Chambers played, it was usually in team sports. His favorite sport was basketball, but he also organized other intramural competitions. He never went out for varsity sports, but he played on several campus-wide championship teams. He would eventually play competitive, USTA-level tennis. His team orientation would stay with him as he built his career, and it would form one of the pillars of his management approach. Chambers the CEO would often brag—and for a man so devoted to the team ideal, it was bragging—that he played only doubles in tennis, not singles, and Elaine would be his partner for regular matches.

Chambers's hard work paid off. He graduated from the West Virginia University College of Business and Economics in 1971 and went on to earn a degree from the college of law in 1974. Later, he would receive an M.B.A. from Indiana University. (Chambers's sisters went on to higher education as well. One became a nurse, the other a teacher—and both of them married CEOs.)

Throughout his life, education would continue to be one of Chambers's passions. His belief in the power of the Internet to carry knowledge and support learning would lie at the center of his vision of a universally interconnected world. In 2000, a group of friends led by his former boss at Cisco, John Morgridge, contributed more than $1.2 million to establish an endowed chair in "Internet Systems" at Indiana University's Kelley School of Business in Chambers's honor. It is one of only a handful of endowed chairs dedicated exclusively to the study of the Internet and related networking systems.

John Chambers continues to maintain strong ties to his hometown, where his parents still live, and to his West Virginia roots. The lessons he learned growing up along the banks of the Great Kanawha River about the value of perseverance and teamwork, combined with his native competitiveness and optimism, formed the foundation of the man and the chief executive he would become.

NOTES

1. Mark Leibovitch, "A Rain God Confronts a Harsh Climate: CEO's Optimism Tested by Downturn," *Washington Post,* April 6, 2001.
2. Geoff Baum, "Cisco's CEO: John Chambers," *Forbes,* February 23, 1998.
3. Jim Balow, "Cisco CEO John Chambers: 2000 West Virginian of the Year," *Charleston Gazette,* December 31, 2000.
4. Ibid.
5. John T. Chambers, "Speaking Up About Dyslexia," *New York Times,* May 16, 2001.
6. Mark Leibovitch, "A Rain God Confronts a Harsh Climate: CEO's Optimism Tested by Downturn," *Washington Post,* April 6, 2001.
7. John T. Chambers, "Speaking Up About Dyslexia," *New York Times,* May 16, 2001.
8. Jim Balow, "Cisco CEO John Chambers: 2000 West Virginian of the Year," *Charleston Gazette,* December 31, 2000.
9. John T. Chambers, "Speaking Up About Dyslexia," *New York Times,* May 16, 2001.
10. Jim Balow, "Cisco CEO John Chambers: 2000 West Virginian of the Year," *Charleston Gazette,* December 31, 2000.
11. Mark Leibovitch, "A Rain God Confronts a Harsh Climate: CEO's Optimism Tested by Downturn," *Washington Post,* April 6, 2001.
12. Jim Balow, "Cisco CEO John Chambers: 2000 West Virginian of the Year," *Charleston Gazette,* December 31, 2000.

CHAPTER 2

SELLING A DREAM

Journalist Andrew Kupfer may have provided the most concise characterization of John Chambers the executive ever to appear in print. In his 1998 *Fortune* profile of the then 49-year-old CEO, he wrote: "He is in overdrive all the time, on a sales call that never ends."[1] That description leaves out a few things—Chambers's personal charisma, his natural optimism, and his focus on people—all qualities that shade and color the manager and the man. But if you had to describe him in a nutshell, professionally speaking at least, you'd be hard pressed to find a better depiction. Former Federal Communications Commission chairman Reed Hundt, who has known Chambers for years, once called him the "most dynamic technology salesman who ever lived."[2] That works, too. But for simplicity, you can't beat the Cisco executive who anonymously offered, "John is always selling."

Chambers the CEO is Chambers the salesman. Customers and colleagues alike describe him as a natural pitchman. He began his career in sales, excelled at it, and found in it a road to success. But that hadn't been his original plan. In fact, until a recruiter from IBM approached him, the thought of taking a sales job had never crossed his mind. It was 1976, and he had just completed his postgraduate studies in business at Indiana University, where he had been president of his class. Now he had an M.B.A. to go with his law degree, and he thought he was meant for better things. "I had no intention of becoming a salesman," he recalled years later. "Why would I waste my education on that?"[3]

His interest in business had been piqued when, as a boy, he worked at a restaurant and motel his father owned in Charleston. That's one of the reasons his law-school studies never led to a career at the bar. What he really wanted was to run his own company. Surely he was better suited to marketing or operations.

But the IBM recruiter, a branch manager named Chris Christie, was persuasive. He painted an almost romantic picture of the work. It was all about solving problems, he said. Understand the technology, and you understand the company's inner workings. Solve a manager's computer problems, and you help his business grow. It wasn't about peddling technology; it was about selling a dream of streamlined business processes and solutions.

Working for IBM, he would be selling computers, and computers were going to change the world. Chambers, who had shown little interest in computing before, was hooked. He found Christie's picture compelling—and he didn't mind that the job gave him an opportunity to make big money—so he signed on for what would turn out to be a six-year hitch. In January of 1977, he and Elaine moved to New York, and Chambers put on the famous IBM uniform: dark suit, white shirt, and conservative tie.

Despite Chambers's eventual disillusionment with IBM's direction in those days, the recruiter's original pitch stayed with him. Today he tells his own employees that they're not in the business of selling technology, but of providing solutions. You are, he tells them, selling a dream.

BIG BLUE

In 1977, IBM was *the* computer company, just as it had been since the 1950s. In those days, bigger was still better, and Big Blue was a big company making the big computer systems called mainframes—the so-called "big iron." (The company's nickname comes from the pale blue cabinets of its early mainframe systems.)

When Chambers joined IBM in 1976, personal computers had not yet arrived on the scene. Steve Jobs and Steve Wozniak had started Apple Computer only a year earlier, but the first Apple machine was still on the drawing board in the Jobs family garage. And Bill Gates and Paul Allen had just founded a little software company called Microsoft.

But there were signs that a change was coming. "Personal computers" had been around for a few years in the form of kits and hobby-level machines. The Scelbi (SCientific, ELectronic and BIological) was based on Intel's 8008 microprocessor chip, which was designed to control traffic lights. It came with 1k of programmable memory and sold for $565. The Mark-8 was a kit computer, also based on the 8008. And the most famous pre-PC era computer, Ed Roberts's Altaire, had made the cover of *Popular Mechanics* magazine. In that 1975 issue, it was described as the "World's First Minicomputer Kit to Rival Commercial Models." That article generated thousands of orders for the computer kit, which shipped with an 8080 microprocessor, a 256-byte RAM card, and the new Altaire Bus design, all for $400. (Of course, the buyers had to put it all together.)

The IBM of nearly three decades ago wasn't quite so light on its feet as it is today. And it didn't have to be; the computer industry was nothing like the turbulent mix of enterprise and consumer markets it would become. *That* IBM sold business computers and typewriters mainly to corporations through a highly structured sales and service system. Consequently, when the new desktop computers emerged as serious business machines in the late 1970s and early 1980s, the company was caught flat-footed.

Chambers watched as IBM, hobbled by an old-economy corporate infrastructure and dated technology, was beaten to the punch by the nimble start-ups of the new PC era. "I learned an awful lot about what not to do," he said in an interview. "You could see management getting further and further from the customer, telling the customer that they knew what he needed better than the customer did."[4]

Big Blue took a stab at the new market for the smaller computers in 1975 with the IBM 5100, but this initial foray was unsuccessful. IBM released the 5100 after two years of development under the code name "Project Mercury." It was the company's first portable computer. The desktop-sized minicomputer wasn't as portable as a modern laptop, but it was smaller than its predecessors. It was considered an entry-level system, which should have made it just the thing for the hobbyists who were swarming to the Altaire. But at $10,000 apiece, "entry-level" was something of a misnomer. A few small businesses and some schools bought the 5100s, but its high-price and modest functionality doomed the device.

In 1980, IBM met for the first time with representatives from a young software company called Microsoft. Big Blue made a deal to license Microsoft's DOS operating system for IBM's new desktop offering, code-named "Acorn." The company reentered the market in 1981 with the Acorn, now called the IBM PC, for the recently coined "personal computer." It was the first desktop box officially called a "PC," and it was the company's first successful offering in the new market. In fact, the IBM PC became an instant industry standard.

The first IBM PC was built with off-the-shelf parts, which opened the market up for clones, a development that nearly buried Apple Computer. It ran on a 4.77-MHz Intel 8088 microprocessor, came equipped with 16 kilobytes of memory, and one or two 160k floppy disk drives. The machines sold for a little over $1,500, and they were sold through third-party distributors (in this case Sears & Roebuck and Computerland. That relationship was a first for IBM.)

The company that had dominated the computer industry throughout the 1960s and 1970s was back. But IBM had come late to this party, and the open architecture of its machines left the door open for other PC vendors to bite into its market. IBM is still one of the world's largest PC manufacturers, as well as a leading provider of software applications and database systems. But other companies, such as Dell, Compaq, and Hewlett-Packard, account for the vast majority of today's PC sales.

During his time at IBM, Chambers worked in sales offices in Indianapolis, Pittsburgh, and Cincinnati. Chambers's competitiveness and relentless approach to sales served him well at IBM, and he became a stellar performer. He learned how to steer customers away from discussions of the technology and to talk instead about business issues. He liked the work, and he was promoted steadily.

But the high-energy salesman found Big Blue's decidedly structured sales system oppressive. While the competition was zipping around the marketplace, IBM's slow-moving and cautious culture was rewarding people for, in Chambers's words, "being status quo."[5] Yahoo cofounder Jerry Yang, another former IBM salesman, once explained the problem this way: "IBM would force the smartest guy on the planet to plod ahead slowly, two years in each job."[6]

Chambers's natural propensity to reach beyond his grasp—to stretch himself with tough goals—seemed to be viewed as a character flaw at IBM. During a performance review, Chambers's manager observed that he had set ten goals, nine of which he met and one of which he missed utterly. Better to set three goals and meet them all, his boss advised. That's when Chambers knew that IBM was not the place for him.

When Chambers left IBM in 1982, he came away with firsthand knowledge of how bureaucracy and conformity could hinder a company in a rapidly changing marketplace. But he left with more than just disappointment. He had spent six years absorbing the company's vaunted sales and customer-service philosophy. The IBM sales organization was a proud group, a real force to be reckoned with, and Chambers liked the camaraderie and the competitive environment that continued to thrive, despite IBM's shortcomings.

The experience also left Chambers with a keen understanding of the importance of the customer. In 1997, he told *Computer World,* "What really [angers me] is when a Cisco employee is arrogant to a customer and says 'I know better than you what you need.' That's what can really get us into trouble."[7]

Years later, Chambers would model Cisco's customer-care philosophy after the one he experienced at IBM.

WANG

In 1983, Chambers left IBM to join Wang Laboratories, the old-line minicomputer powerhouse based in Lowell, Massachusetts. There he found a mentor in the company's founder, Dr. An Wang. Chambers has described his former boss as the smartest man he ever met, and one of the finest people he ever knew.

An Wang was one of the pioneers of the early computer industry. He came to the United States in 1945 from his hometown of Shanghai, China, to study at Harvard University. He had earned his B.S. degree from Chiao Tung University in Shanghai in 1940, and at Harvard he earned a Ph.D. in applied physics.

In 1948, Dr. Wang invented magnetic-core memory, which dramatically boosted the capabilities of mainframe computers. It became the most common technology used for storing computer data before the invention of the integrated circuit. Wang's "Pulse Transfer Controlling Device" would be one of his best-known contributions to the computer industry.

IBM bought Wang's patent for his memory core in 1951 for $500,000. With this money, he launched Wang Laboratories in a Boston loft. Although the company has faded from the high-tech spotlight, overshadowed by the host of hot technology firms and big-brand names that followed, Wang was once one of the most recognized and successful companies in the computer industry. In 1988, Dr. Wang was inducted into the National Inventors Hall of Fame, alongside Edison, Pasteur, and Bell.

Wang started the company to develop and commercialize specialized electronic devices, many of which were his own inventions. During his lifetime, he would secure more than thirty-five patents for computer-related technologies. One of his early contracts was for the first electronic scoreboard, which was installed at New York's Shea Stadium.

The company's first big commercial product was a desktop calculator system, which the company began making and selling in the early 1960s. It was about the size of an electric typewriter, and all it could do was add, subtract, multiply, and divide. Simple as the machine was by today's standards, it had great commercial success and fueled the company's initial growth.

By the late 1960s, Wang Labs was beginning to market a supercalculator the size of an electric typewriter. It had roughly the capabilities of a modern programmable pocket calculator and used a small cassette tape recorder to store data and programs.

In the 1970s, Wang became one of the world's leading suppliers of word processors and minicomputers. The newly emerging word-processor market was huge, and Wang's machine led the transformation of the modern office. The Wang Word Processing System sent the company's sales soaring to $3 billion by 1988. For the first time, typewriters began giving ground to a new device for creating and processing documents.

Minicomputers, or "minis" as they were called, fell somewhere between a PC and a mainframe in terms of size and capacity. They were usually stand-alone computer systems with attached terminals and other devices. Minis were precursors of what are today known as servers. Wang sold its minis to small and midsize companies for general business applications and to larger businesses for department-level operations. Wang, along with DEC, was among the top minicomputer makers in the industry.

In the late 1980s, Wang moved into the development of an integrated optical storage office-networking system based on the then-new IBM PC standard. By that time, Dr. Wang had developed cancer, and his son, Frederick Wang, took over as company president.

When Chambers joined Wang in 1982, the company enjoyed a near-monopoly in the word-processing business, and its minis were threatening the dominance of IBM's mainframes. He worked at Wang for eight years, first as vice president of the company's central regional U.S. operations and later as senior vice president of Wang's Americas/Asia-Pacific operations.

During his time at Wang, Chambers performed as he had at IBM, turning in "world-beater" numbers. But the 1980s PC revolution caught the company by surprise, and its revenues soon went into a steep decline. The advent of the PC drove the Wang word processor right off the desktop, utterly replacing it in just a few years.

At the center of the word-processing systems were the company's own VS minicomputers and their proprietary operating systems. Although the company continued to sell its minis, it stuck with his own proprietary software, even as cheaper machines running the Unix operating system that had now become an industry standard began to catch on. Chambers watched as Wang's refusal to let go of its proprietary systems cost the company its competitive edge in the mid-1980s.

In 1989, Wang was generating $2 billion in profits; a year later, it would post a $700 million loss. The advent of the PC had made the company's minicomputers obsolete, leaving it (and every other minicomputer maker) without a product. In the industry, the phenomenon is known as category destruction.

As the market for Wang's products began to dry up in the late 1980s, Chambers was looking for strategies to cope with the radically changing environment. The solution he employed was both simple and practical: He found a partner—a contract manufacturer to build PCs that would carry the Wang label. It was an approach that Chambers would later refine at Cisco, where he would keep his company technologically competitive through a strategy of acquisitions.

But Wang wasn't the only company failing to adapt to changes sweeping the industry. Digital Equipment, Unisys, and Data General, along with IBM, all faced the same unexpected shifts in demand, and they all reorganized in some fashion to develop new products.

Chambers was running half the company's overseas businesses when, late in 1990, Dr. Wang himself asked him to return to the States and take over U.S. operations. Chambers initially thought he would be taking over his new responsibilities sometime in the new year, but his boss had a big job for him that couldn't wait.

NEVER AGAIN

During the final days of 1990, Wang's new executive vice president would oversee the layoff of five thousand employees. Chambers spent the holiday weekends planning the layoffs. It was the worst job he'd ever had to do, and the process made him physically ill.

Chambers has spoken often of the Wang layoffs. In 1999, during an appearance on ABC's "20/20," Chambers talked about the experience with Diane Sawyer: ". . . what happens that tears you up is, often, when the layoffs occur—we like to call it downsizing, but it really is layoffs—it's during a time when finding another job is very difficult. And so, you look people in the eye and you realize that you're wrecking their lives and their families . . . it about killed me . . . I couldn't have done it another year." Chambers's father told Sawyer, "He was miserable. He would call home, and we would talk about it, talk to his mother as well as to me, just explaining how difficult that was for him to do."

After the layoffs, Dr. Wang named former General Electric executive Richard W. Miller to top management, effectively pushing his son Frederick out of the company. Miller then succeeded to the chairmanship after An Wang's death in 1990.

By that time, Chambers had had enough. He chocked up his decision to leave to a loss of confidence in the company's leadership. To be sure, Wang's future was in serious doubt. The company's decline would lead to more layoffs, losses totaling $116.3 million two years later, and Chapter 11 bankruptcy. But Wang did emerge from bankruptcy as a provider of services and applications for networks—a very different company, but one that would double in size between 1994 and 1997. The company got a boost in 1995, when Microsoft Corporation agreed to invest $90 million in Wang and to incorporate Wang's imaging technology into Windows 95. Microsoft planned to incorporate Wang's office automation and workflow technology into Microsoft Exchange, a rival to Lotus Notes. Wang would eventually realize annual revenues of $1.3 billion.

But it was most likely the layoffs that were the last straw for Chambers. Firing so many people, and sending them out into what was then a tough job market had been a dreadful experience that undoubtedly soured him irrevocably on the company. Finally, in December 1990, Chambers left Wang with no particular prospects, but vowing never to face such a layoff again.

NOTES

1. Andrew Kupfer, "The Real King of the Internet," *Fortune,* September 1998.
2. Mark Leibovitch, "A Rain God Confronts a Harsh Climate: CEO's Optimism Tested by Downturn," *Washington Post,* April 6, 2001.
3. Andy Serwer, "There's Something About Cisco," *Fortune,* May 2000.
4. Andrew Kupfer, "The Real King of the Internet," *Fortune,* September 1998.
5. Mark Leibovitch, "A Rain God Confronts a Harsh Climate: CEO's Optimism Tested by Downturn," *Washington Post,* April 6, 2001.
6. Marshall Loeb, "The IPO Boom: How to Make $400,000,000 in Just One Minute," *Fortune,* May 27, 1996.
7. Bob Wallace and Maryfran Johnson, "Cisco CEO: John Chambers," *Computerworld,* November 3, 1997.

CHAPTER 3

MEANWHILE, WAY OUT WEST: THE FOUNDING OF CISCO

Back in 1984, when John Chambers was still working at Wang Laboratories, nearly a decade before he would find himself at Cisco, the Internet as we know it today didn't exist. Its progenitor, ARPANET, had only recently begun using TCP/IP, the networking protocol that would become the de facto standard for computer communications. And Tim Berners-Lee's multicolored, multimedia World Wide Web was still years away.

But the personal computing revolution was in full swing. IBM had introduced its first PC in 1981. In 1983, the year *Time* magazine named the microcomputer its "man" of the year, a one-year-old Compaq Computer Corporation made its initial public offering. (Microsoft's IPO was two years away.) Apple Computer had been ahead of the pack with its first three offerings—Apple I, Apple II, and the Lisa. In 1984, Apple made history with its unveiling of the Macintosh during a one-time-only broadcast of its famous "1984" commercial, which ran during that year's Super Bowl. It was the first computer with a mouse and a graphical user interface, and it sold like hotcakes—50,000 units within 75 days of the announcement, according to the company.

But computer *networking*, was just beginning to emerge as an industry. In 1984, groups of computers, mostly in academic settings, were connected by small, local area networks (LANs). The networks themselves, however, were still relatively isolated from one another—except at Stanford University, just up the road from Apple headquarters, near Palo Alto, California. There two staffers had woven the university's disparate networks into a single, unified system. Late that year, Sandy Lerner and her husband, Len Bosack, would leave their Stanford jobs to start a company that would utterly dominate an emerging market and pave the way for the Internet boom.

THE LEGEND (SLIGHTLY AMENDED)

The legend of the founding of Cisco Systems is a Silicon Valley classic: Sandra K. Lerner and Leonard Bosack met in graduate school, fell in love, and married. After graduating, they took jobs managing computer networks located at different corners of the sixteen-square-mile Stanford campus. They longed to exchange romantic e-mail, but their networks were incompatible. Sandy supervised the computers at Stanford's graduate school of business, while Bosack worked five hundred yards away at the computer science lab.

Both networks were based on Ethernet technology, originally developed at the Xerox Palo Alto Research Center, better known as PARC, and given to Stanford for free. PARC researchers Robert Metcalfe and David Boggs invented Ethernet. (In 1979, Metcalfe founded 3Com, a company that would become one of Cisco's greatest data-networking rivals.) But Bosack's network was made up of PCs, whereas Lerner's department used DEC minicomputers. And the systems spoke different languages. Lerner has described the Stanford computer world in those days as a tower of Babel.

To solve their problem, Lerner and Bosack built bridges to connect the networks, and then built devices called routers to manage the flow of bits. Lerner talked about the Stanford project in 1998 with columnist-author Robert X. Cringley for the PBS documentary "Nerds 2.0: A Brief History of the Internet": "We basically pulled wires through manholes, we pulled wires through sewer pipe. We built a lot of things by ourselves. It was very much a guerrilla action at that point. We certainly didn't have any official sanctions. In the end, I guess the University is allowed not to like it, but they did get a network out of it."

Their first routers were crude boxes, but these were improved as the network project progressed. A "router" is a piece of hardware and software—a specialized computer, really—designed to manage communications among computer networks. Routers ship information around the networks in packets, which are chunks of data, separately addressed. The routers read the addresses for the packets and transmit them via the most expedient path. Those boxes were the key to the whole thing.

If they ever did, Lerner and Bosack no longer claim to have invented the router, and have repeatedly acknowledged the role of others in its development. In particular, Bill Yeager, who was then an engineer at the medical school (and now a senior software architect at Sun Microsystems), seems to have played a pivotal role in the router's evolution.

Tom Rindfleisch, director emeritus of the Lane Medical Library at the Stanford School of Medicine, calls Yeager the principal inventor of the multi-protocol router. In 2000, Rindfleisch published a letter on the Stanford University web site in which he sought to set the record straight about who invented this device. In his letter, Rindfleisch wrote that Yeager was assigned the task of connecting the two networks that Lerner and Bosack managed and that they were helped by Kirk Lougheed, who would later join the couple at the fledgling Cisco. Rindfleisch wrote:

> By June 1980, a PDP11/05-based router was in place, which connected the medical school and department of computer science. By 1981 Yeager developed a unique network operating system, which would be the basis for the MC68xxx version of the code. This was completed later that year, and was ultimately licensed by Cisco

> Systems . . . Thus, by [the] time Bosack had access to the router source code in 1985, multiple-protocol routers were a relatively mature technology.[1]

In other words, Yeager wrote the original version of the software that allowed routers to act as translators among different network media or protocols. Lerner and Bosack did secure a license for that software in 1986 from Stanford University's Office of Technology Licensing, and Yeager was named in the license as the principal developer/inventor. He reportedly received 85 percent of the royalty distribution, which Rindfleisch claims he pumped back into a Stanford networking project, but none of the credit. He writes:

> Bosack's and Lerner's contributions lay in the important (and risky) realization that this technology could be made into a commercial venture, and credit for that should not be denied. Still, Yeager never benefited from that venture, nor was he given an opportunity to by the organizers of Cisco Systems. Nor has he received public recognition for his major contribution to Cisco's founding and success.[2]

Rindfleisch took Cringley to task for his telling of the story in the "Nerds" documentary. Cringley (the nom de plume of technology journalist Mark Stephens) published Yeager's version of events on his Web site (www.pbs.org/cringely/pulpit/pulpit19981210.html). He also published Kirk Lougheed's comments on the subject, which read, in part:

> I consider the standard story of Len Bosack and Sandy Lerner developing networking and routing at Stanford as something akin to a sound bite. It sounds good, but hides a lot of complexity. As anyone who has been around Silicon Valley for a while knows, there are a lot of people besides the founders who are critical in the creation of a company. However, in the story-telling business, a complex story is a snoozer, so lots of details—and people—get dropped from the story. Good marketing people and other myth makers under-

stand this; Cisco's early marketing people are largely responsible for the standard Len and Sandy story.

On the subject of who created its franchise technology, the company Web site explains simply that Cisco was founded in 1984 by a group of computer scientists from Stanford University.

Eventually, the network Lerner and Bosack helped to create would connect Stanford's then five thousand computers. With the network up and running, Lerner and Bosack approached the university about making the router technology available to others. But when Stanford balked at the idea, they decided to pursue it themselves with an independent commercial venture.

SANDY AND LEN

Given Stanford's historical role in fostering technology ventures, it's surprising that the university showed so little interest in commercializing technology that was developed on its campus. Stanford is the mother beast of many Silicon Valley creatures, and technology transfer is a real watchword at the university. Hewlett-Packard, Varian, Sun Microsystems, and a host of other high-tech brand names grew out of research carried out at, or supported by, the university. In 1938, Fred Terman, Stanford's first professor of electrical engineering (the first one anywhere), reached into his own pocket to loan William Hewlett and David Packard $538 to develop their first device, an audio oscillator, which they put together in a Palo Alto garage. (That garage has become such an icon that Hewlett-Packard paid $1.7 million for it in 2000. The current CEO, Carly Fiorina, used it as a backdrop for a series of television ads. The owners threw in the house for free as part of the bargain.)

Sun Microsystems was founded in 1982 by Stanford students Vinod Khosla, Andy Bechtolsheim, and Scott McNealy, along with Berkeley professor Bill Joy. The company's name is an acronym for Stanford University Network, the campus-wide wide area network (WAN) on which

Lerner, Bosack, Yeager, and others worked. Much later, Bechtolsheim would join Cisco Systems.

And it's not as though Lerner and Bosack weren't members of the home team. They both earned graduate degrees from Stanford in 1981. Lerner received a master's in statistics; Bosack earned a master's in computer science.

In 1997, Lerner recalled in an interview how she met Bosack at the Stanford computer lab when they were still students: "Nerd culture at Stanford was pretty extreme. There was no way I could have taken one of these people home to meet my family. But Len's clothes were clean, he bathed, and he knew how to use silverware. That was enough. I was enchanted."[3] For Bosack, it was Lerner's intelligence and sense of humor. She was bright and quick, and he was smitten.

The couple married in 1980. Lerner's recollections notwithstanding, Bosack wasn't the only geek in the family. According to one story, the couple talked in a kind of shorthand "nerdese." Lerner would say "Control-D!" when she wanted Bosack to shut up. ("Control-D" is a computer keyboard delete command.) In their new enterprise, Bosack would be the technical guy—Lerner's Woz; she was the Jobs of the duo: intense, ambitious, and driven.

After a frustrating name search, the couple decided to call their new company "cisco," after nearby San Francisco. Originally, the initial "C" was lowercase; it was capitalized beginning in 1995 because so many newspaper and magazine reporters and editors complained about it. Lerner created the company's now-famous logo to resemble the Golden Gate Bridge. (The rise to prominence of another company with a similar sounding name, Houston-based SYSCO Corporation, which delivers meals to hotels, schools, and hospitals, prompted John Chambers to joke during a 1999 speech to a group of Charleston business leaders, "My mother still thinks I'm working for the food service industry.")[4]

At first, Lerner and Bosack set up shop in the house they shared with Bosack's parents in suburban Atherton, California, just up the road from Stanford. They bought a used mainframe and set it up in the garage. One bedroom served as the lab, another bedroom was turned into office space, and they used the living room to build and test. They hired friends, maxed out their credit cards, and took their initial orders over the nascent Internet.

Cisco Systems shipped its first products in March 1986. Initially, its customers were other universities and research centers—people who had heard about the routers via ARPANET, on the pre-Internet geek grapevine. There was no money for advertising, and there was no sales staff, so the young company developed its customer base strictly by word of mouth. Throughout its first decade of operation, small "c" Cisco grew at an average rate of more than 200 percent annually. Until 1992, the company never paid a dime for advertising. They didn't need to.

Although they were taking in about $250,000 a month, and the company was actually making a profit, Lerner and Bosack were desperately short of cash. Lerner went back to work for a while as a corporate data-processing manager to bring in some money, and the couple began approaching venture capitalists.

SILICON VALENTINE

Silicon Valley's Sandhill Road area is home base to most of the world's venture capitalists, literally, and for many years most of the world's venture money was invested within a few miles of that Menlo Park, California, neighborhood. But in 1986, venture funds weren't as abundant as they would become in the 1990s, when all you needed to secure funding was a ".com" after your name. Lerner and Bosack were turned down repeatedly. Donald Valentine at Sequoia Capital was the 77th moneyman they approached.

Why so many venture capitalists (VCs) had turned the company down might have had something to do with their perceptions of the eccentric founders. In a 1995 *Fortune* interview, Don Valentine said that he and his partners at Sequoia invested in Cisco in spite of some real reservations. "Ninety-nine percent of venture capitalists think of themselves as investing in great people," he said. "In this case, we looked right past Len and Sandy, and concentrated instead on the great potential market that existed for their product. . . . They were good scientists, and did a lot to set the tone for the company, but they had never managed a thing."[5]

Lerner has admitted that she and Bosack started the company without much of a business plan, but with a sweeping technical vision. Even so, the young company was a going concern. At the time Valentine invested, Cisco was pulling in around a quarter of a million dollars every month. Len and Sandy's ragtag team had built that business without a professional sales staff or traditional marketing campaign. Cisco had both a solid product and real revenues. It conducted nearly $1.5 million worth of business in 1987 and turned an actual profit of $83,000. The company had begun to expand its customer base to include lucrative corporate clients like Philips Electronics.

Lerner has said that the money and management expertise Sequoia provided her company were much needed and welcome, but she and Valentine clashed from the beginning. "Don's first words to me were, 'I hear you're everything that's wrong with Cisco,'" Lerner told Robert Cringley. She reportedly shot back that she was the reason there *was* a Cisco.

But Valentine was a big-time VC with a remarkable Silicon Valley pedigree. He was one of the founders of National Semiconductor, and had served as a senior sales and marketing executive at legendary Fairchild Semiconductor. In 1972, he founded Sequoia Capital, and he was one of the original investors in Apple, Atari, LSI Logic, Oracle, and 3Com.

And he did want to invest in Cisco—he saw enormous potential in computer networking—but he wouldn't do it without some big concessions from the founders. They would have to give up control of the company and let Valentine handpick and hire a professional management team, what Valley VCs jokingly call "adult supervision."

In exchange for Valentine's $2.5 million investment—the only infusion of venture capital the company would ever need—Sequoia Capital would receive close to one-third of the company's stock, and Valentine would become the chairman. Lerner and Bosack retained 35 percent of the stock, but their control of the company was greatly diminished. Among the concessions made was to give Valentine the authority to recruit management and to develop the company's management process.

The key draft pick for Cisco came in 1988, when Valentine hired John P. Morgridge to serve as Cisco's first CEO. The 55-year-old Stanford graduate was then president of Grid Systems, a struggling laptop maker. But Morgridge was looking for other opportunities, and a headhunter put him in touch with Valentine.

Lerner didn't meet Morgridge until after he'd already been hired. Whatever their initial exchanges, everyone could see that tensions between Lerner and the new boss were high from the beginning of their association. And things would only get worse. Morgridge later recalled that Lerner and Bosack "were basically selling to their peer group, through word of mouth. The initial customer set started with the lunatic fringe—the kind of people who are way out on the leading edge. The early people were very technical and tolerant. There's been a big shift in who uses the product."[6]

Under Morgridge, Bosack became CTO, and Lerner's new job was running Cisco's customer-service group, which she called "customer advocacy." (It was a name that would stick with the organization.) But she chafed under the new regime. A former employee recalls that she and Morgridge quarreled constantly, and that Lerner often stormed ranting and raving into the offices of the new executive team members.

Until Valentine hired Morgridge, the Cisco staff had been made up of Lerner and Bosack's family and friends. Valentine brought in real professional management, and the new, buttoned-down environment was tense. "I think I was very frustrated but [Len] was kind of quieter about it," Lerner said in a 1997 interview. "The venture people were into building a bigger business and we were into building the best networking computer that you could build. They're not the same."[7]

Valentine, Morgridge, and the executives they hired were, indeed, out to build a bigger company—that's bigger with a "B," as in billions.

Cisco had a real jump on the burgeoning computer-networking market, and routers were a hot item in the late 1980s. The new management team took full advantage of their lead. Sales of the company's products grew from $1.5 million in 1987 to $28 million in 1989. On February 16, 1990, the company went public. The price of Cisco's IPO stock was $18.00 a share.

The IPO made Lerner and her husband rich, but they weren't happy in the new organization. Lerner was particularly miserable. As the company grew, Valentine added management, leaving her further and further out of the loop. She has said that she found herself screaming about a lot of things during that period. It seemed to be the only way anyone would listen. "I'm guilty," she said in a 1995 interview "of standing in someone's office and not taking no for an answer when a customer needed something done."[8]

Terry Eger, Cisco's first head of sales, has said that Lerner became very difficult to deal with. Later that summer, when she allegedly yelled at one of the company's big customers, Eger and the other execs made up their minds to address the situation. A group of seven of the company's new vice presidents met with Valentine. With Morgridge's knowledge, they gave the chairman an ultimatum: Either Lerner goes or we do.

On August 28, Lerner was asked to leave the company. Morgridge and Valentine reportedly tried keeping Bosack, but he left after hearing the news of his wife's ouster. The couple sold their two-thirds stake in Cisco almost immediately and walked away with $170 million, leaving billions on the table. Neither has publicly expressed any regret over their decision, and Lerner has said that she didn't want her money tied up with people she didn't like.

Years later, Morgridge, in characteristically blunt language, would offer this perspective on events: "This was a cottage industry that was populated by friends of the founders. And while many were enthusiastic, most had no particular competency in the area they were working in, including the founders. So, in those early days it was kind of like joining a family. And families are not always open and receptive."[9]

LIFE AFTER CISCO

Lerner and Bosack left the company with millions, but the business had taken a toll on their marriage, and they soon split up. Lerner blames years of overwork, financial struggles, and making the company a priority instead of the marriage. Although they are divorced, by all accounts the parting was amicable, and they remain friends. In fact, together they used a reported 70 percent of their money to establish the Bosack/Kruger Foundation, a charitable foundation. ("Kruger" is the "K" in Sandra K. Lerner.) Through this foundation, they financed a wide range of animal welfare and science projects. Both Harvard and Stanford have received funds from the foundation, as have the Center for Wildlife Conservation and the SETI (Search for Extra Terrestrial Intelligence) Project. It also paid for a 125-year lease on the four-hundred year-old Chawton House, the Hampshire, England, manor just up the road from the cottage where Jane Austen lived and wrote during the last eight years of her life. Lerner's plan was to turn the dilapidated fifty-room manse into the Chawton House Library by 2003. When completed, the nonresidential study center will house Lerner's collection of over six thousand early English novels by women.

In 1991, Bosack founded XKL Systems, a privately funded communications-engineering company based in Seattle, Washington. Not much information is available about the company as of this writing, but according to its very sketchy Web site (www.xkl.com) "XKL explores and develops new approaches and architectures for the communications industry."

Lerner's post-Cisco history is a bit more colorful. In January 1996, she launched Urban Decay, a Mountain View, California-based alternative cosmetics business. With the tag line "Does Pink Make You Puke?," the company offered shades of lipstick and nail enamels in unorthodox colors with names like Pigeon, Asphyxia, Toxin, Gangrene, Mildew, and Bruise. The company counts among its customers pro basketball player Dennis Rodman and actress Drew Barrymore. Urban Decay products have found their way into Nordstrom, Neiman Marcus, and, in London, Harvey Nichols. Lerner later sold her stake in the company. She also bought Ayrshire Farms, a nearly eight-hundred-acre spread in Loudoun County, Virginia, and stocked it with animals. That farm is the site where she famously posed for a photographer from *Forbes* magazine, nude, astride her favorite horse.

Years later, there seemed to be no lingering hard feelings at Cisco toward the unique couple who started it all. In 1994, to commemorate the tenth anniversary of the founding of the company, Cisco endowed the Leonard Bosack and Sandy K. Lerner Professorship at Stanford University. Named, according to Stanford's publicity office, to honor the company's two founders, it supports faculty members working at the forefront of information systems technology in computer science, electrical engineering, or a related field.

NOTES

1. Tom Rindfleisch, "Origins of Cisco Systems—The Real Story," Stanford University, 1999.
2. Ibid.
3. Dana Wechsler Linden, "Does Pink Make You Puke?" *Forbes,* August 25, 1997.
4. "Cisco Systems Seeks Better Recognition of Internet Role," The *Charleston Gazette,* May 11, 1999.
5. Joseph Nocera, "Cooking With Cisco," *Fortune,* December 1995.
6. Julie Pitta, "Long Distance Relationship," *Forbes,* March 16, 1992.
7. Garrett Glasser, "Cisco Co-Founder Finds New Path," MSNBC, November 21, 1997.
8. Joseph Nocera, "Cooking With Cisco," *Fortune,* December 1995.
9. Jennifer Reese, "View from the Top," *Stanford Graduate School of Business Magazine,* 1996.

CHAPTER 4

HEIR APPARENT

John Chambers left Wang Laboratories in 1990 with no immediate job prospects. He spent his first unemployed month sending out résumés that generated no interviews. Undaunted and with characteristic optimism, he reached out to old friends and came up with nearly two-dozen leads.

Among those he contacted was a former colleague from Wang, Terry Eger, who was Cisco's first head of sales. Eger's description of the small networking company out in California hooked Chambers. Even though Cisco had only $70 million in sales and was minuscule compared to IBM, Chambers was excited about the opportunity.

John Morgridge had been running the company for a couple of years when he and Don Valentine interviewed Chambers for a senior sales position. Lerner and Bosack had moved on, and the company had gone public the year before. Although Morgridge had made no announcements, the 57-year-old chief executive was looking ahead to the time when he would step down from the day-to-day operations of the company. He hired Chambers with the understanding that he would eventually be running things.

NERDVANA

Chambers had been to some exotic places since he had left West Virginia fifteen years earlier—New York, Boston, the Far East—but he'd never been anywhere quite like Silicon Valley. Physically, it was a ten-mile-wide stretch of land bordered on its southeastern edge by San Francisco Bay and sheltered on its northwestern side from the Pacific Ocean by the Santa Cruz Mountains. The climate was moderate, often described as Mediterranean, and the sun shone much of the year.

In her book *Silicon Valley: Inventing the Future,* Jean Deitz Sexton wrote that trying to describe Silicon Valley "is like trying to get your arms around an elephant as it's jogging down the road. The Valley is physically immense, ethnically diverse, and in constant flux, driven ever forward by the force of technology. . ."[1]

Intellectually—and, one might say, spiritually—it was Nerdvana, Geektopia, The Valley of the Propeller Heads, home to more Ph.D.s per square mile than anywhere else on earth. It was the very epicenter of the global high-tech tsunami, where the personal computer had been born in a garage and nerds were treated like rock stars. It was also Type-A-ville, where eighty- to one-hundred-hour workweeks were common, and programmers kept sleeping bags tucked into their cubicles for quick naps between all-nighters. But it was no company town (*towns,* actually). You could scratch virtually any code jockey, marketing rep, or first-year M.B.A. candidate and expose a nascent entrepreneur. Local high-tech enterprises commanded the lion's share of *all* venture capital dollars. In fact, if you weren't starting up your own company, helping someone else start up his or her own company, or at least *thinking* about starting up a company, people began to worry that you weren't getting enough protein in your diet.

Dressed in what would become his trademark dark suit, white shirt, and muted tie, Chambers fairly glowed with the aura of *IBM*. In the entrepreneurial meritocracy of Silicon Valley, established old-line technology companies like IBM had been the enemy, your father's company, a place where individuality was squashed and conformity ruled. All of that had been discredited in the land of T-shirt millionaires. The perception of success had changed. Some people in Silicon Valley went to work without *shoes,* never mind a necktie.

Worse, Chambers was a salesguy. The superstars of Silicon Valley were engineers and programmers. They were out in the garage *inventing* things. Cisco itself still harbored a core of Stanford supergeeks who weren't impressed by Chambers's M.B.A. or J.D. degrees. For them, salespeople were a necessary evil.

SCROOGE

Of course, the company's CEO was a former salesman himself. Morgridge shared none of the prejudices of the tech-centered. He once said, "Salesmen usually end up being president of the company, so if you want to be president, it's not a bad place to start."[2]

There were other striking parallels between his and Chambers's lives. Both men had grown up in the suburbs, although during very different times. Morgridge spent his childhood in Wisconsin during the Thirties and Forties, in a southeastern suburb of Milwaukee called Wauwatosa, a child of the depression (which may account for his celebrated thriftiness).

Both men had earned M.B.A.s and married their high-school sweethearts. Morgridge met his future wife, Tashia Frankfurth, while they were students together at Wauwatosa's East High School. Like Chambers and Elaine, Morgridge and Tashia attended college together. After graduation, they moved to Madison to attend the University of Wisconsin. They both graduated in the spring of 1955 and were married later that summer. Elaine Chambers became a speech pathologist and Tashia Morgridge a special-education teacher after earning her master's degree.

After college, Morgridge spent three years in the air force. While he was in the service, an IBM salesman sold him on the idea of a career in the computer business (the same thing that had happened to Chambers nearly twenty years later). After being discharged from the military, Morgridge—like Chambers—took a job as a sales rep.

Until 1980, Morgridge worked for Honeywell Information Systems; he then joined Stratus Computers as the company's marketing vice president. In 1986, he was hired as president of Grid Systems, a job he has described as dreadful. "Companies have personalities," Morgridge said in a 1996 interview. "Have you ever met someone for whom, no matter how they live, life is always trouble? That was Grid. Every day I'd come home and my wife would say, 'What happened today?' And something had always happened. A supplier crapped out. The government put a 100 percent duty on flat plasma screens. It was endless."[3]

By the time Tandy Computer purchased Grid in 1988, Morgridge was ready to move on. In personal presentation, Morgridge and Chambers were worlds apart. Both wore traditional business suits (unlike so many of Silicon Valley's "T-shirt millionaires"), but Chambers affected the IBM uniform. He was—and is—very polished. Morgridge has been compared to television's Columbo, and accused of buying his suits at a box discount warehouse. It's well known that Chambers takes lots of time to prepare for press interviews and analyst presentations. He never shows up without a thick binder and hours of preparation. Morgridge was known for his off-the-cuff frankness, which included a penchant for the occasional profane utterance. "If you don't want to hear the answer," Chambers once said of Morgridge, "don't ask the question."[4]

And, of course, there's the legendary Morgridge frugality, and the story about Chambers's first experience with this aspect of his new boss's personality: Soon after he began working at Cisco, Chambers turned in his first expense report. The report came back, the story goes, with the short-term parking expenses circled and a coupon for long-term parking stapled to it. Morgridge had written his name on the coupon. This oft-told story notwithstanding, Chambers has often disputed Morgridge's frugal image, describing him as an exceptionally kind and generous person.

Don Valentine, another Silicon Valley executive famous for his thrift, has declared that Morgridge is the only president he has ever backed who is cheaper than he is. "And I am very cheap," Valentine said. "One of the things I was warned about when we were doing reference checks [on John] a long time ago was that when you have dinner with him, don't let him choose the wine. I've always carefully heeded that advice."[5]

But Morgridge is proud of his reputation. He's the one who laid the foundation of Cisco's cost-conscious culture. From early on, the company was known and admired for its prudent spending practices. Everyone knows that Cisco executives don't fly first class, and that includes the CEO. And Cisco City (as the company headquarters in San Jose are known) is spare and utilitarian. Everyone works in twelve-by-twelve offices. Again, even the CEO. Morgridge believes a company's values radiate from the top. Throughout his tenure at Cisco, he regularly topped those lists of the lowest-paid CEOs. "You can't have double standards," he said in a 1996 interview. "Someone flies first class, no one else does; he gets a suite, no one else does. You can run the company that way, but don't expect employees to be excited about it. Particularly now, because companies are so much flatter. The positive impact of the electronic world is that you can create a worldwide culture; the negative is, when we tried to make do with 24 flavors of pop, it lasted one week, and there was all this e-mail about second-class citizenship and 'how come we can't have Snapple?' There's very little that's not known."[6]

Morgridge was referring to what he has called the "soda pop issue." According to a former Cisco employee, the founders provided their people with free beverages. After they left the company, Morgridge tried to scale back that little perk by reducing the selection of free drinks. The employees went ballistic. According to Morgridge, "It shut the place down." The lesson for Morgridge: Never let your employees get used to any perk you might want to take away someday.

His tight spending policies notwithstanding, Morgridge was no Scrooge. Under his auspices, Cisco earned a reputation for philanthropy that continues to rival its high-tech peers today.

SUCCESSION

Three years after starting at Cisco as the company's senior vice president of U.S. operations, John Chambers was promoted to executive vice president with responsibility for research and development, manufacturing, worldwide sales, marketing, and support. He was now, for all intents and purposes, the number-two man, and would be working closely with Morgridge and the senior management team.

When *Computerworld*'s Paul Gillin asked Morgridge about his retirement plans in a 1994 interview, the 61-year-old chief executive was uncharacteristically evasive. When Gillin asked him how much longer he intended to stay on as CEO of Cisco, Morgridge replied, "It's not my intent to stay that long. Ten years is too long to be with one company these days. One of the great things about Silicon Valley is that we're not a single culture. We're a collection of cultures. Chaos and change is very important to the lifeblood of the company."[7] When asked directly whether he had chosen a successor, Morgridge said, "We've recently made some moves to broaden Chambers' responsibility. That should tell you something."[8] He told another reporter who asked about his retirement plans, "I do have retirement plans, my wife has plans, and they don't always agree." When asked directly whether he had chosen a successor, Morgridge said, "We've recently made some moves to broaden Chambers's responsibility. That should tell you something."[9]

But the CEO's plans were really no secret. In July of 1994, just a few weeks before the company closed its books for the fiscal year, Cisco Systems held its first-ever analysts' meeting. Although Chambers was still the number-two man, he dominated that meeting. It was clear to everyone in attendance that he was Morgridge's heir apparent and was probably making most of the day-to-day decisions.

In 1993, Morgridge had surprised Cisco's board with the announcement of his intention to retire in two years. The board tried to convince him to stay. At the time, Don Valentine commented that Morgridge was the best president in the business, and he was committed to doing whatever it took to keep him on.

But Morgridge had made up his mind and recommended Chambers as his replacement. Although some on the board worried about Chambers's sales background, most liked his self-effacing personal style and his deference to Morgridge. He seemed to be very comfortable with Morgridge's basic business plan. Here was an executive who wasn't going to fix something that wasn't broken; he wasn't going to change things just for the sake of changing them. And after all, hadn't Morgridge come from a sales background himself?

Chambers was named CEO in January 1995. By then, the message was unequivocal: John Chambers was brought into Cisco with the expectation that he would eventually run the company. In a press release issued at the time, Morgridge said, "Over the past four years his responsibilities have been steadily increased and during the last eighteen months John has been pivotal in the execution of Cisco's decentralization plan and acquisition strategy, key components for the company's overall long-term growth, and acquisition strategy."

John Morgridge once described his company's business as tying all the horsepower in the computing business together. Under his management, Cisco had become the largest and most profitable computer-networking company in the world. During his tenure, he took the company public and grew the operation from $5 million in sales to over $1 billion and from 34 employees to over 2,260. When he handed the reigns to Chambers, the company was on a stellar trajectory, and he was confident that Chambers would take the company to the next stage in its development.

After stepping down, Morgridge stayed on as chairman of the board. Don Valentine, who had served as chairman since 1988, became vice chairman. Chambers had been strongly influenced by Morgridge, and he would leave much of what the former chief executive had put together at Cisco in place. But it wouldn't be long before the transplanted West Virginian would begin leaving his own mark on the company. In early 1996, using Hewlett-Packard as a model, Chambers divided Cisco's 150 products and 4,400 employees into six teams. And, following in the footsteps of another CEO he admired, General Electric's Jack Welch, he established what would prove to be a fundamental tenet of his leadership: From now on, Cisco would not seek to compete in a market unless Chambers and his team believed that they could capture the number-one or number-two spot.

NOTES

1. Jean Dietz Sexton, *Silicon Valley: Inventing the Future,* Windsor Publications, 1992.
2. Jennifer Reese, "View from the Top," *Stanford Graduate School of Business Magazine,* 1996.
3. Ibid.
4. Ibid.
5. Ibid.
6. Ibid.
7. Paul Gillin, "Cisco Sees Switching in Its Future," *Computerworld,* August 15, 1994.
8. Ibid.
9. John Labate, "The Battle for Your PC Network," *Fortune,* October 31, 1994.

CHAPTER 5

COMPETITION AND CONVERGENCE

Almost from its inception, the volatile data-networking industry forced companies to adapt fast to remain competitive. The same thing might be said about many segments of the high-tech sector, but in networking things have always been especially lively. Unlike other powerhouse technology companies, such as Microsoft and Intel, which enjoyed near-monopoly status virtually from birth, Cisco Systems has operated in an environment rife with serious competitors. The company may have gotten the drop on the competition with its early commercialization of the router, but as the demands of network traffic increased, the market for network equipment and software would prove to be a rapidly evolving space. Start-ups with hot technologies and a handful of big players would keep Cisco on its toes. This was an environment in which the highly competitive John Chambers would thrive.

PC-IFICATION

In the early days of computing, the desktop unit was a "dumb" terminal, connected to a centrally located mainframe, where shared applications and data resided. But the arrival of the personal computer in the early 1980s brought with it a decided shift in the computing landscape.

PCs and the more powerful desktop machines, called workstations, were slipping through the backdoor of the enterprise, eroding the old model of large, shared computing systems. The new stand-alone machines offered performance and cost benefits that sophisticated power users working in corporate information technology (IT) departments simply could not ignore. For them, at least in the beginning, these new PCs offered unmatched individual productivity.

But decentralized computing—or what Bay Networks' CEO, David House, once described as the PC-ification of the networking industry—had its downside. Stand-alone machines might improve an individual's productivity, but work-group productivity often suffered. PC and workstation users couldn't share files or printers, and they were cut off from the traditional corporate computing environment, since, although PCs may have been taking over, the old systems didn't just go away. It quickly became clear that, valuable as they were, the desktop machines would be much more of an asset to an organization if they were connected.

Before the advent of this PC permeation, there wasn't much of a need for an independent networking industry. Until the microprocessor hit the desktop and began to push computing away from the centralized model, the big computer system companies had supplied their own communications hardware and software. It was proprietary stuff, but back then IT departments preferred homogeneous technology; platform independence wasn't yet the gold standard it would become in the age of the Internet.

But that situation was quickly changing. "More and more PCs were being deployed in business," IDC analyst Ken Presti explained to me, "but the companies needed to make them talk to one another. Computers that were connected were inherently much more valuable."

Local-networking protocols, such as Ethernet and Token Ring, were emerging to support locally linked groups of PCs into LANs (Local Area Networks). More than 60 percent of the nearly 50 million PCs deployed in 1994 were wired to networks within companies, universities, and hospitals.

New technologies appeared to link the LANs into WANs (Wide Area Networks), and new companies formed to exploit them, in the process creating a new data-networking industry, independent of the old-line computer system vendors. Systems vendors, such as Hewlett-Packard, Digital, and IBM, which had been the de facto data-networking leaders, were soon surrendering their market dominance to companies specializing in the hardware and software that moved data among disparate machines and networks.

THE BIG FOUR

In the early days of data networking, there were a slew of small players, but a kind of merger mania gripped the industry between 1989 and 1994. During that period, the data-networking industry saw 129 mergers and acquisitions. In the aggregate, these transactions totaled more than $4 billion.

Initially, mergers and acquisitions served largely as a defensive tactic employed by the industry leaders to fend off the upstarts and each other. Even as Cisco was poised in 1994 to begin an unprecedented seven-year acquisition campaign, Morgan Stanley's Bill Brady would write:

> While we continue to witness a large number of promising startups developing new technologies (switching technologies, ATM, etc.), we believe a far greater percentage of this crop will choose to merge with the networking establishment than was the case with prior generations.[1]

In 1994, Cisco was a leading member of the networking establishment. This was the year the company's revenues surpassed the billion-dollar mark, its market cap approached $10 billion, and it joined the ranks of the Fortune 500. Cisco, and its rivals 3Com, Bay Networks, and Cabletron Systems, were considered the big four of data networking. Together they controlled about 80 percent of the market by the late 1990s.

Chambers has said that he looked at his competition back then in terms of the big eight, which also included Newbridge Networks, Ericsson, and the separate entities that formed Cabletron, Wellfleet, and Synoptics. "We broke away from those guys in about four years, and we broke away largely by using our own systems and a lot of people still don't get that," Chambers said in a 2001 interview. "We saved more money than our nearest traditional competitor. What they were spending on R&D we were putting back in R&D. If Cisco can't beat them doing that then we are never going to win."[2]

Networking-equipment maker 3Com Corporation was Cisco's oldest competitor. Founded in 1979 by Robert Metcalfe, the former Xerox engineer who had helped to create the Ethernet protocols that linked the computers in Sandy Lerner and Leonard Bosack's local networks at Stanford, 3Com grew into a formidable data-networking company. The three "coms" in the company's name, which would one day adorn a football stadium in San Francisco, stood for "computer," "communication," and "compatibility."

In 1997, 3Com and market-leading modem maker U.S. Robotics agreed to merge. At the time, it was the largest merger in the history of the data-networking industry. The $6.3 billion merger created a company nearly as big as Cisco, with a broader product line. Rochester, New Hampshire-based Cabletron was another of Cisco's elders, but not by much. Just a year older, it was founded in 1983 in a garage as a part-time venture. By 1996, it had evolved into a billion-dollar company. A fierce competitor for years, Cabletron had a very different culture from Cisco's. Chambers described the company's management team as street fighters for whom he had a lot of respect.

At the end of the summer of 2001, Cabletron completed a "corporate transformation strategy" that spawned four new companies: Global-Network Technology Services, a network-consulting firm; Enterasys Networks and Riverstone Networks, which operate as fully independent public companies; and Aprisma, which operates as an independent subsidiary of Enterasys. Cabletron ceased to exist as a separate public company.

The youngest of the big four was Bay Networks, which was formed in 1994 through a merger of Santa Clara, California-based SynOptics Communications and Wellfleet Communications of Billerica, Massachusetts. The merger created a billion-dollar company that provided routing, switching, ATM, remote access, and sophisticated network management from a single vendor. The founders chose the company name to reflect the locations of the two companies: the San Francisco Bay Area and the Bay State. At the time of the merger, SynOptics was the number-one hub vendor and Wellfleet was the number-two router provider. Cisco had considered a merger with SynOptics earlier that very year but instead acquired Crescendo Communications, which they thought would be a better fit, culturally and technologically.

In the market dominated by these companies, small start-ups didn't have much of a chance on their own. Data networking's big four had by then built up massive installed customer bases, and they had invested heavily in the development of sophisticated sales and service channels. Even with hot, in-demand technologies right in their hands, it had become too expensive and too risky for many start-ups to go it alone.

And for many, there was actually little incentive to try. The IPO had long been the high-tech start-up's preferred "exit strategy." Now, *acquisition* presented an alternative path to success for the industry's entrepreneurs, as well as a new source of R&D for its established leaders.

And as the vendors in this market changed, so did the preferences of their customers. Buyers of networking software and equipment, who had for years been perfectly happy to pick and choose among a range of vendors for "best of breed" components, were beginning to look to companies with broad product lines and big-time market coverage. Again, Brady made the case back in 1994:

> Ironically, the success of network management and internetworking has provided MIS managers with the tools to push the pendulum back in their direction, and look for vendors with complete solutions, instead of making a selection from the best of what is out there. Now able to interconnect, analyze, and manage complex

> global networks, MIS managers are beginning to demand that networking companies supply them with broader solutions that have global service capabilities.[3]

Big was good, and the magical "end-to-end solution," the pursuit of which would become John Chambers's personal mission, seemed to be exactly what people were looking for. But the scope of that solution would be expanding soon. Within two years the networking industry would begin a new cycle of changes—and Chambers saw them coming.

"While all this was going on," IDC analyst Presti says, "Chambers was telling us that he was less concerned about Bay and 3Com than he was about Lucent and Nortel. He was looking far enough down the road that he could see convergence, and he saw that the major telecom players were going to have an important role in this. That was his position as far back as 1996." John Chambers, it seems, was ahead of the curve.

A HYBRID UNIVERSE

In the early days of computer networking, it was all about moving data. Bits and bytes traveled around on their own specialized networks, on hardware and software built by data-networking companies. Voice traffic traveled through the telephone system—the other network—but never the twain did meet.

All that changed with the ascendance of the Internet. People first began making phone calls through cyberspace via advertiser-supported, free telephone services, in the mid-1990s. The quality of the calls was low, but the system enjoyed a measure of popularity, especially among international callers. The new buzzword in networking was "convergence," and the convergence of voice and data would pit data-networking companies against telecom companies in a new, hybrid universe.

At the center of this hybrid universe was IP (Internet protocol) telephony, also referred to as Voice over IP (VoIP). (Over intranets, or WANs, the process is usually known as VoIP; over the Internet, it's most often called "Internet telephony," but the terms are often used interchangeably.) So-called circuit-switched networks, such as the phone system, wasted bandwidth with dedicated circuits that were never fully utilized. But packet-switched networks, such as the Internet, which used IP, utilized every microsecond of bandwidth by sealing bits of voice data into packets, several of which could be routed along the same circuit simultaneously. IDC's Presti explains it this way: "In a regular phone call, we basically have two lines that allow us to talk at the same time—which is why we don't have to say "over" when we talk on the phone. In that system, a lot of the infrastructure is not in use at any given time. While I'm talking, you're listening, and vice versa. You go into a packet-based network, and the information—your voice—is shipped around in electronic envelopes. It's more like the US Postal Service than it is a phone line. And it's much more cost efficient."

At the same time, that data traffic was exploding with the advent of the Internet, and modems were beginning to connect people to computers via the telephone system, telecommunications companies were replacing century-old networks of copper wires originally designed simply to carry only phone calls, with astoundingly more powerful optical fibers.

Optical fibers that transmit light waves had been around since the 1970s, but it wasn't until the 1980s that companies figured out how to send information through those fibers. They do it by dividing light waves into channels and then packing data into each channel. The effect in a single channel has been compared to a lightbulb going on and off ten billion times a second, flashing the 0's and 1's of binary computer code down the fiber.

In an optical-fiber-based network, strands of glass carrying pulses of light convey trillions of bits per second. A single, hair-thin strand of fiber provides bandwidth equal to a copper bundle as thick as a wrestler's neck. This new network of light is more reliable, more secure, and able to span longer distances without repeaters to regenerate fading signals.

The phone companies have been revamping the telecom infrastructure for years, replacing many miles of copper wire with optical-fiber cables. By the end of 1990, roughly eight million miles of fiber had been laid in the United States. A decade later, more than eighty million miles of the glass strands would crisscross this country, with a total of 225 million miles laced across the globe.

But planting the new wires—"laying the glass"—wasn't cheap. It was going to cost East Coast telecom NYNEX Corporation and its partners a reported $1.4 billion to lay the 17,000 miles of fiber optic cable between London and Tokyo in 1995 (before its merger with Bell Atlantic). Expensive price tag aside, most experts agree that, eventually, copper wires will be replaced entirely by optical fiber. Consultants at Renaissance Worldwide in Newton, Massachusetts, have predicted that the capacity of this country's long-haul fiber-optic network could grow from a system that can handle 126 billion simultaneous phone calls to one that can handle 54 trillion in 2001.

TAKING ON TELECOM

By 1997, Cisco had all but cornered the data-networking space. The company not only dominated its traditional routing market, but it had also taken the lead in high-end LAN switches. The company's growth was topping 80 percent, and its net income had doubled.

To continue growing the company at the phenomenal rates to which investors were becoming accustomed, Chambers would have to look to new hunting ground. And so he focused in on telecom—a $700-billion-a-year industry in the midst of a vast makeover. In doing so, he faced a new "big eight": Alcatel, Siemens, Sycamore, Sienna, Redback, Foundry, Lucent, and Nortel. But he knew that it was Lucent and Nortel that he had to beat, and beating them would take some doing. When Chambers began turning his attention to telecom in earnest in 1998, Nortel was twice as big as Cisco, and Lucent was three times larger.

Lucent Technologies was, and still is, the leading maker of telecom equipment in the United States. The company was a spin-off of AT&T,

and many of its products were developed at the legendary Bell Laboratories. Based in Murray Hill, New Jersey, the company can trace its history back to the 1800s from the original Western Electric Company, to American Bell Telephone, to AT&T.

Close on Lucent's heels was Nortel Networks, the world's second-largest telecom-equipment maker. Based in Brampton, Ontario, Canada, Nortel makes switching, wireless, and optical-network systems for telephone carriers and other communications service providers. Formerly known as Northern Telecom, it also has a storied history that goes back to the 1800s, all the way back, in fact, to Alexander Graham Bell himself.

Reportedly, Chambers considered the possibility of forming alliances with Nortel and Lucent in 1998, but no deals were ever struck. According to Cisco, neither company was willing to give up its share of the market for high-speed switches, which Cisco had been dominating. At the time, Chambers said that a partnership with either company would have been too much of a culture clash. "Lucent is trying to compete in a New World environment when they're an Old World company in terms of the rules of the Internet economy," he said.

In 1998, the Federal Trade Commission (FTC) looked into allegations that Cisco had colluded with Lucent and Nortel, its two biggest rivals. The FTC soon dropped its investigation, but Cisco now looks to preempt such government action. Cisco general counsel Dan Scheinman has met with Justice Department officials to explain why Cisco shouldn't be considered a monopoly. Even as Microsoft continues to battle the government on similar issues, Cisco seems to have slipped from the Justice Department's clutches—at least for now. It is likely, however, that the monopoly hunters will continue to keep Cisco in their sights.

Cisco scored a coup in 1999 when it announced an agreement with telecom giant Qwest Communications to develop one of the largest IP-based networks in the country. Under that agreement, more than 80 percent of Qwest's telecommunications services would move to Cisco-built networks. The companies would also codevelop applications for Internet-based data, phone, and image services.

A year later, Chambers scored again when Sprint announced its decision to have Cisco build its combined voice/video/data network. At that time, Cisco was ranked among the six largest telecommunications companies in the U.S. Until the announcement, Sprint's major supplier had been Nortel.

In September 2000, Cisco furthered its VoIP goals by entering into a joint venture with Internet telephony company, Net2Phone. Together they formed Adir Technologies to "productize" a network management platform developed and used by Net2Phone. The Unix-based Adir Management Platform (AMP) can monitor all the major elements of a VoIP network, including gateways; gatekeepers; and the origination, routing, and termination of calls. Net2Phone is a leading player in IP telephony. At the time of the Cisco deal, the company claimed a 40 percent market share, with an estimated 95 percent of its business coming from charges for Internet phone calls. Through Adir, Cisco became a supplier of network management software to providers of telecommunications, wireless, and broadband Internet services.

Cisco's foray into telecom lit a fire under the established equipment manufacturers. Chambers didn't, as a matter of company policy, move into markets where he didn't believe he could dominate, or at least capture second place. And he was known in his industry as a man who did not like to lose. If Cisco had decided to go after the traditional telecom carriers, the established vendors were in trouble.

The dominant players on the voice side went on buying binges, acquiring companies with expertise in data networking. Lucent paid $1 billion for Yurie Systems, an ATM equipment manufacturer, and also purchased Ethernet start-up Prominet and remote-access-equipment maker Livingston Enterprises. Nortel bought data-networking start-up Aptis Communications, and, for $9.1 billion, acquired Bay Networks, one of the big four data-networking companies. And French telecom giant Alcatel acquired DSC Communications for $4.4 billion, which gave it a foothold in the United States.

"Everyone right now is looking to be an end-to-end player and setting themselves up to be a strong competitor in the emerging market," Craig Johnson, principal of the consulting firm The PITA Group, said in an interview at the time. "The Ciscos will migrate to support voice at the same time the Lucents will get the pieces they need to compete on the data side. The snowball is starting to pick up speed."[4]

UPSTART

Throughout 1998, Cisco's lead in its bread-and-butter router market went virtually unchallenged. Then an upstart in nearby Mountain View, California, founded by some former Cisco execs and managers from its closest competitors, blew the company's doors off.

Founded in 1996, Juniper Networks is a next-generation networking company that builds high-end routers and other equipment for telecom carriers that are reorienting their networks from voice to data architectures. The company was started by seasoned execs from the data-networking market. Its CEO, Scott Kriens, was one of the founders of StrataCom, which Cisco acquired in 1996. The CFO was Marcel Gani, former CFO of Grand Junction Networks, also acquired by Cisco. The vice president of engineering, Peter Wexler, was a former VP of engineering at Bay Networks. Both Joe Furgerson, the start-up's director of marketing, and Gary Heidenreich, its VP of operations, were 3Com expatriates. And Steven Haley, the VP of sales, had that same role at both StrataCom and Cisco.

Since its formation, Juniper has steadily eroded Cisco's router market share. In 1998, Cisco owned a greater-than-90-percent share of the router market; by 2001, Juniper had wrested 30 percent of that market away, and the company's market valuation had reached $16.7 billion.

BURGEONING BANDWIDTH

By 2000, the proliferation of optical networks, and the scramble among networking vendors to provide hardware and software capable of exploiting the faster speeds that such optical networks allowed, had precipitated an explosion of bandwidth. But how much of that fiber was actually being "lit," the industry term for strands in use? In 2001, the industry began to hum with talk of a bandwidth glut. All this fiber had opened up the information highway, but many of the lanes were still empty, and expectations about the traffic boom were overstated, or so went the talk.

"Fiber laid isn't the same as fiber lit," wrote Grahame Lynch in a 2001 article published in *America's Network.* Lynch, who is the author of *Bandwidth Bubble Bust: The Rise and Fall of the Global Telecom Industry,* wrote:

> It's not about bandwidth glut; it's about the ability to really do something with that bandwidth. If there's a bandwidth glut, then the logical assumption is that bandwidth is getting commoditized, so now you have all this abundance of bandwidth, but what do you do with it? I think the applications will be there.[5]

In 1999, by some estimates, less than 5 percent of the capacity of all the fiber then in place was in use. Surely, part of the problem was the expense. In 1999, for example, IXC spent an estimated $1 billion to install fifteen thousand miles of fiber-optic cables, 24 to 48 fibers thick. The company expected to light just two to four of those fibers immediately following the completion of their installation. Lighting the rest of them would cost about $10 billion—money that IXC just couldn't afford to spend. Around the same time, Telecom carrier Qwest was estimating that it would cost their company as much as $13 billion to fully light all of its unused fiber.

But lower-than-expected demand was more likely the root of the problem. "For Qwest, Level 3, and all of us to light our networks to the max would be silly," IXC's CFO James Guthries said at the time. "The demand isn't there." Industry watchers began to speculate that the growth of optical networking would be considerably slower than expected, depending on the pace of demand.

By 1999, it was clear that Chambers believed it was going to be an IP world. He has often talked about a "New World Network" that would expand from the Internet to encompass computers, telephones, and even home appliances. With Cisco's dominance in data networking, that particular future was looking very bright.

And he was right about at least one thing: As voice increasingly becomes just another form of data on the network, virtually every telecom carrier has integrated IP to provide converged voice and data services. The major carriers control their own Internet backbones, so they can implement VoIP that approaches the quality of a normal telephone call. Most industry watchers expect IP to become the universal transport for all voice, data, and video communications worldwide.

Despite the economic downturn of summer 2001, traditional voice carriers, Internet service providers, and new competitive network providers continued to converge, building through their actions end-to-end networks that will carry voice, data, and video.

NOTES

1. Bill Brady, "Consolidation in Networking," *Red Herring,* November 1, 1994.
2. Paul Briggs, "Interview: Cisco Chief John Chambers," *Computer Reseller News,* April 20, 2001.
3. Ibid.
4. John Geralds, "The R&D race is on as market switches on to value of optical communications," VNUNET.com, July 9, 1999.
5. Grahame Lynch, "The media still misses the bandwidth glut point," *America's Network,* June 1, 2001.

CHAPTER 6

THE CUSTOMER IS THE STRATEGY

John Chambers delights in telling the story of his first meeting as president and CEO with the board of directors of Cisco Systems. His account in a 1996 interview with *Upside* magazine's Eric Nee is particularly vivid:

> The board was supposed to meet at 9 o'clock, and I was heading out of my office at two minutes to nine, when a call came in from a customer, who had a problem and wanted to talk to me. My first reaction was to hand the call off to my vice president of customer services, customer advocacy. This was my very first board meeting, and it was very important to me. But I was no more than three steps down the hall when I realized that, as important as this first board meeting was to me, I wasn't setting the kind of example I wanted to set as president. I turned around, went back to my office, and took the call. I was 20 minutes late to my first board meeting, and they were unhappy about it, but you have to walk your talk.[1]

When Chambers finally arrived at the meeting, nearly half an hour late, his new board was not happy with him. This was not an auspicious start. But when Chambers told them why he was late, they quickly excused him and agreed that their new CEO had his priorities right where they wanted them. Chambers would often joke that he now had an excuse if he was ever late again.

CUSTOMER CONSCIOUSNESS

Cisco Systems has been described as the most customer-focused company in high tech. Perhaps it's just that Chambers preaches the doctrine of customer satisfaction more fervently than any other CEO in the business. Either way, it's an odd distinction. It's sort of like saying that a doctor is very patient-focused, or a coach is very player-focused. How on earth could a company—any company—*not* focus on its customers?

The tech sector is a quirky place, however, where engineering-heavy organizations run a real risk of paying too much attention to the technology itself and not enough attention to the people they expect to buy and use it. There is in this marketplace a kind of techier-than-thou arrogance that renders a surprising number of technology-driven companies unresponsive to their customers. Worse, it is an attitude that can go unchallenged because an equally surprising number of companies with cutting-edge technologies have achieved genuinely big wins with little or no customer consciousness.

Chambers is no engineer, and that sets him apart from many of his peers. Critics argue that Chambers's non-techiness is a weakness in an executive whose job it is to guide and protect the fortunes of a leading-edge technology company. Some say that he is, in fact, *too* focused on his customers, that he listens to them too much, and that his approach has left Cisco too dependent on them. They say that this dependence has produced a "whipsaw" product strategy. (A Cisco competitor once compared the company's product catalog to a telephone directory.) This, his critics charge, is no way to innovate.

Of course, Chambers isn't interested in innovation per se. The failures at IBM and Wang that so impressed and distressed him as a young executive—missteps he vowed never to repeat—were not failures to innovate, but rather failures to execute effectively. Chambers is not here to invent a better mousetrap but to run a profitable company, and that job is all about building lasting relationships with customers.

Cisco is an applied-technology company, not a basic research organization, and its CEO is a salesman. Chambers is a people person. Tinkering with the technology is not his forte, although he is intimately familiar with his company's product line and technical direction. His strength lies in his ability to connect with customers, to understand their problems, and to do everything in his power to encourage them to continue doing business with Cisco—that, and his single-minded dedication to convincing everybody that they should be doing business with Cisco.

And yet, there is some truth to what his critics say. The company Web site is rife with verbiage affirming that Cisco depends on its customers to point the way to future product and service offerings. Chambers has often gone outside his company for the tech du jour his customers tell him they want. He has made acquisitions based on customer recommendations—he bought Crescendo Communications and NetSpeed because of customers' counsel. It's a strategy that leaves the company particularly vulnerable to the mercurial demands of its customers, which can lead to ill-advised acquisitions. Chambers himself has conceded this last point.

Still, he makes no excuses for his approach. In fact, Chambers contends that Cisco's heavy reliance on customer feedback is one of his company's strengths. He believes that Cisco's success depends on open customer communication, and he has fostered a corporate culture that continues to be deeply committed to listening to its customers. Cisco does not fall in love with its technology, Chambers has said on many occasions. It builds what its customers say they want. This is a strategy that began with Cisco's founders and blossomed under Chambers' leadership.

"BASED ON PAST EXPERIENCE"

Sandy Lerner was just as obsessed with the company's customers back in the 1980s as Chambers is today, and arguably planted the seeds of customer consciousness early in the company's history. Cisco was originally something of a geek clubhouse, with no sales force at all, but Lerner always looked after customers. For her treatise on the links between Stanford University and local industry, Carolyn Tajnai talked with Lerner about the subject. "[We] had a highly unusual, skilled, intelligent, and motivated initial customer base," she told Tajnai "which essentially directed our engineering efforts. It is the customers who are the one, key ingredient in the [C]isco success. It's a shame companies lose sight of who they should try to please."[2]

But Chambers has certainly kicked things up a notch. The CEO focuses on customer issues with laserlike intensity, reportedly spending more than thirty hours a week with customers. He's known for his practice of listening to at least ten voice-mail messages from Cisco staffers in the field reporting on the status of top accounts every night before he goes to bed. In the morning, he personally reviews as many as fifteen "critical" accounts. And he often calls on customers himself when there's a problem that needs to be solved.

If he pays this kind of attention to customers, Chambers reasons, everyone else in the company will, too. It is a strategy that seems to be working. Reportedly, the customer focus runs right down through the organization—even to the engineers.

And Chambers does seem to be willing to move heaven and earth for his customers. According to one apocryphal story told to me by several people, a customer from Finland who was visiting Cisco's San Jose facility became ill and had to be hospitalized. Chambers flew the man's family to California, and then, unsatisfied with the care he was receiving, moved him to a different hospital.

Chambers's fixation on customer satisfaction is almost certainly a consequence of his experiences at his two previous jobs. A Chambers quote posted on the company Web site is revealing in this regard. It reads:

> Customer satisfaction is a personal top priority, and I fully expect it to be a top priority for everyone who works at Cisco. Based on past experience, I've learned the value of remaining focused on customer needs.

"*Based on past experience.*" Chambers has diplomatically left "at IBM and Wang" out of that sentence, but it is implicit and obvious to anyone who knows his story. Chambers watched as his former employers lost customer confidence and consequently suffered losses in rapidly changing markets. Their chief sin, Chambers has said time and again, was that they lost track of their customers. For IBM, it was a big stumble in the PC market that nearly left the company in the dust; Wang's missteps led to bankruptcy.

Chambers is not one to repeat mistakes, his own or anyone else's. Neither is he one to throw the baby out with the bathwater. Although IBM slipped up early in the dawn of the PC age, the company that Chambers worked for nearly three decades ago had one of the world's most powerful and effective sales organizations on the planet. He has, in part at least, modeled Cisco's customer-care philosophy on the IBM of thirty years ago.

THE SURVEY

In 1992, Chambers took a fairly drastic step to foster a strong customer satisfaction orientation throughout his company. That year, Cisco began tying the results of a customer-satisfaction survey conducted independently by an outside organization to employee compensation. Cisco employees now receive a yearly bonus that is tied to the performance of the company as a whole. For upper-level people (that is, every Cisco manager, from the person on the shop floor to the CEO), that bonus can account for more than one-third of their annual earnings. And the fate of one-third of that bonus rests on the results of the survey. If a manager's scores on the survey improve, he or she gets more; but if they decline, the money comes out of the manager's pocket.

Cisco's Annual Customer Satisfaction Survey allows Chambers and his management team to measure and test whether they are walking their talk. It might be thought of as a kind of private Nielsen rating for the company. An independent research firm conducts the survey, which polls Cisco customers via an Internet-based questionnaire, and then analyzes the results. Typically, customers from all over the world respond, using a five-point satisfaction scale (5 for "very satisfied" through 1 for "very dissatisfied") to grade the company on about sixty performance criteria. The survey seeks to quantify customer satisfaction with the company's products, services, support, and field sales. It poses questions like, "If you were making your internetworking vendor decision today, who would be your first choice?"

The results of each survey are made available to Cisco employees and partners via the Web. In 2001, Cisco reported receiving an overall grade of 4.48. That survey drew more than 30,000 responses, which was more than double the responses from the previous year. (And which is not surprising, considering how often the company was in the headlines that year.)

If any of the news from the survey is negative, the company sets up focus groups and conducts follow-up surveys to get to the root of the problem. Cisco conducts a similar survey to measure customer satisfaction with the company's so-called channel partners.

Cisco is one of the very few tech companies to establish such a direct link between customer contentment and employee earnings, and Chambers is often dismissive of other enterprises that claim to do the same thing. He has said that when people talk about being customer-focused, the first thing he asks is whether their reward system is tied to the customer's success. He says that he has found, almost without exception in his industry, that the answer to that question is no.

But the company's voracious appetite for customer feedback could never be satisfied by an annual survey or even focus groups alone. Every Cisco customer service rep learns to ask customers random questions about how the company might do things better. Chambers himself is constantly trolling for feedback about himself and his company. He's always looking for what he calls reality checks. And he'll solicit them from just about anybody. When *Wired* reporter Joe Flower finished his 1997 interview with the CEO, Chambers turned the tables on the reporter. Flowers wrote:

> I've used my allotted hour, I'm packing up the PowerBook, then he stops me. "Wait a minute," Chambers says. "I'm not going to let you off that easy. You've been doing this a long time, you've looked at a lot of companies, you've been looking at ours pretty hard for a while. So tell me: What can I do better? What am I missing? What advice can you give me?"
>
> The question is far from casual. We crank on it for half an hour. He really wants to know what I think. Is this just the ultimate journalist seduction ploy? Maybe. But it's also a very good one, and what strikes me is that I have interviewed hundreds of CEOs and not one has ever asked me what I thought.[3]

CUSTOMER CZAR

Well-managed customer relationships continue to be integral strategic components of Cisco's business plan. The roots of the company's intense focus on these relationships go very deep. When Don Valentine and John Morgridge assumed the management of the company in the late 1980s, cofounder Sandy Lerner took on a new role. She established the company's first customer-support group, which she called customer advocacy.

In 1991, Douglas C. Allred would reprise that role as Cisco's senior vice president of customer advocacy. His primary responsibility was, not surprisingly, to ensure customer satisfaction and to smooth the rollout of Cisco's technology through support services. Before the company's restructuring in summer 2001, one in five Cisco employees worked within the customer advocacy organization. Allred was something of a pioneer in his particular corner of the high-tech universe. He oversaw the changes in Cisco's compensation model that tied managers' paychecks to customer satisfaction. And he championed Cisco's implementation of an enterprise resource planning system (ERP) to improve order fulfillment.

When, in the early 1990s, the company's internal surveys revealed that customers were increasingly dissatisfied with Cisco's order-fulfillment process, which had an average lead time of twelve weeks, Allred advocated the implementation of a new Oracle ERP system. Cisco had the system up and running with characteristic alacrity—it reportedly took the company only eight months; most companies needed thirty-two. The warp-speed implementation of the new software played havoc with Cisco's finance, manufacturing, and customer-service organizations. But following its implementation, Cisco was able to knock order fulfillment lead time down to three weeks or less.

Allred's role on Cisco's executive team has also been called Chief Customer Officer, or CCO, and sometimes "customer czar." As of this writing, some IT industry mavens were already wondering whether the CCO might not prove to be a fad that would go the way of the Chief Knowledge Officer and Chief Quality Officer. But companies in general were becoming more customer-centric—and many were seeing a brighter future for the CCO, including industry analysts at Meta Group and Gartner, both based in Stamford, Connecticut. A Meta report anticipated that, by 2003, a quarter of all global 2000 businesses would have a CCO or its equivalent. Gartner analysts expected 15 percent of U.S. companies to have a customer czar by the end of that same year. At Cisco, thanks in no small part to Chambers's own core values, the position was an integral part of the organization. In fact, the company's customer service, product design, and IT groups all report to customer advocacy.

Even the IT department at Cisco reports directly to customer advocacy, so that technical projects are tightly matched with customer service. This close interaction between IT and customer advocacy is key to the company's ability to keep its customers loyal and happy. Giving the customer czar jurisdiction over IT, as Cisco did, served to spread the King Customer code throughout every layer of the company. Consequently, the information services department at Cisco is as customer-centric as the rest of its operations.

The arrangement also steered the company's information services people away from strictly internal projects. Everyone should ask, went the code, How will this help the customer? It was that kind of thinking that transformed what would have been little more than an internal order-tracking tool for Cisco employees into a Web-based system that allowed customers to place orders, download software, and get technical support online. (More on this subject in Chapter 10.)

Such hyper-awareness can make for a jittery corporate culture, and that's probably okay with Chambers, at least where the customers are concerned. He has often joked that he wants to cultivate a culture of paranoia at Cisco. He has described his company as more paranoid than Intel's Andy Grove, author of the book *Only the Paranoid Survive.* According to his employees, Chambers isn't exaggerating.

"The paranoia thing is true," a former employee told me. "We could never just sit back and say, Hey, we're number one. Our managers used to tell us that we were about two years away from being put out of business by the competition. They wanted us to think about it, constantly."

Employees wear the phrase "Dedication to Customer Success" attached to their ID badges. "He's trying to make us all think we're salespeople," another employee says. "I can't tell whether that's a good thing, or a bad thing, but he's sure done a great job of it."

NOTES

1. Eric Nee, "Interview with John Chambers of Cisco Systems, Inc.," *Upside,* July 1, 1996.
2. Carolyn Tajnai, "From the Valley of Heart's Delight to the Silicon Valley: A Study of Stanford University's Role in the Transformation," Stanford University, 1996.
3. Joe Flower, "The Cisco Mantra," *Wired,* March 1997.

CHAPTER 7

GROWTH BY ACQUISITIONS

When John Chambers assumed the role of CEO in 1995, the then little-known company had a market cap of around $9 billion. At its peak in March 2000, Cisco was worth $555 billion and was, albeit briefly, the most valuable company in the world. In those five-plus years, Chambers presided over the creation of more than $480 billion in stockholder value and expanded the company into nearly every part of the networking industry.

Even by Silicon Valley standards, that was an eye-popping growth curve. Chambers didn't so much grow his company as launch it like a rocket into the networking industry's stratosphere. (In a now well-known company training video, a Cisco employee looks at the camera and actually says, "Working at Cisco is like being strapped to a rocket. It never stops.") The fuel powering that rocket was a growth-by-acquisition strategy that allowed the company to thrive in a world of truncated product development cycles and rapidly shifting technology, where speed and innovation were absolute competitive necessities.

Cisco made its first acquisition in 1993, while Morgridge was still running the show, and had a total of four under its belt by the time Chambers took his place two years later. By 1997, the company had completed a total of twenty-one acquisitions, and the strategy was getting a lot of positive attention. In 1998, the company added nine more enterprises to its acquisitions list. In 1999, Chambers and company added twice that many. And in a kind of climax characterized frequently that year in the business press as a "buying frenzy," 2000 saw twenty-three new companies brought into the fold for a total of sixty-nine acquisitions under John Chambers. But, in 2001, Chambers slammed on the breaks. As of August of that year, Cisco had acquired only two new companies. The grand total as summer drew to a close: seventy-three.

Until the U.S. economy took a southward turn and the bottom dropped out of the tech sector, Cisco's acquisition strategy was lauded by analysts and envied by competitors. As far as investors were concerned, that strategy had turned Cisco's stock into the closest thing they had ever seen to a sure bet. Until the bad news got worse in the spring of 2001, it seemed to almost everyone that Cisco's ability to acquire the technology it needed had put Chambers in the driver's seat of a genuine moneymaking machine.

"He [Chambers] did an amazing job of taking the company from an obscure, very heavily technical little niche player out in the Bay area, to a stock in every major mutual fund manager's portfolio," Glenn Rifkin, co-author of *Radical E: From GE to Enron, Lessons on How to Rule the Web,* told me "Under Chambers, the company went from the 800-pound gorilla to the 8-million-pound gorilla in its market sector."

But who's strategy was it? Rifkin, who also covered Cisco for the *New York Times,* gives Morgridge credit for playing a key role in the beginning, and he credits the acquisitions team that included Charles Giancarlo, Mike Volpi's predecessor, with brewing the initial process. But it was Chambers, he says, who made acquisitions a keystone of the company's growth structure and a tenet of the corporate culture.

"Chambers clearly took the acquisitions strategy and made it the center piece of the growth of this company," Rifkin says. "Chambers saw that this was a way to effectively grow the company, and he embraced it, big-time. He was the visionary behind the company's growth."

In many ways, the strategy was a manifestation of the man. In 1993, the year of Cisco's first acquisition, the company was still what one insider described as a "techie cult." Chambers was the sales guy, the "suit," the WVU grad in a nest of Stanford supergeeks. He was technologically agnostic—just like Cisco's routers—free of the inhibitions of a surprisingly large number of executives who refused to truck with technology they hadn't developed in-house, free of the "not-invented-here syndrome" (better known locally as "NIH"), free to see the big picture.

In the world that Chambers saw before him, NIH was a potentially fatal malady. He had no love of technology for technology's sake, Chambers would often tell reporters over the years. He wanted to play across the entire internetworking marketplace. To accomplish that goal—to become in the networking world what IBM was in the mainframe market, and Intel and Microsoft are today to PCs—he would have to challenge some outdated but entrenched ideas about growing a high-tech company.

In a 1997 interview, Chambers told Rifkin that he and his colleagues made a conscious decision to attempt to shape the future of the entire industry back in 1996. That was the year of Cisco's first acquisition, which wrought some major philosophical changes at the company. Chambers told Rifkin:

> We decided to play very aggressively and truly attempt in the networking industry what Microsoft did with PC's and IBM did with mainframes. If you think of networking as the fourth evolution of computers—the first being mainframes, where IBM dominated; the second, minicomputers, where there was no clear leader; and the third, personal computers and local area networks, which was the era of Intel and Microsoft—and if you understand that each evolution is bigger than the prior generation, you begin to get an idea of what we saw in front of us.[1]

CRESCENDO SETS THE STAGE

In 1993, Cisco was the undisputed router king. The company had sold 124,000 of the devices, and would sell millions more over the next few years. But the advent of the Internet and the growing popularity of enterprise intranets had created a networking boom, and traffic was piling up. Routers were still a hot item, but they were slow compared with some of the newer technologies, and some new companies were emerging to satisfy the rapidly rising need for speed.

Two technologies in particular had the potential to outsell routers: switching and asynchronous transfer mode (ATM). ATM was still in the experimental stages of its development, but switches were more cost effective as Ethernet LAN hubs than Cisco's routers, and they had the potential to cut seriously into Cisco's business.

Chambers has often told the story of the day the gravity of the coming market changes hit him. It happened during a visit to the offices of longtime Cisco customer Boeing. The news was bad. Very bad. Boeing executives told Chambers, then senior vice president of worldwide operations, that he was about to lose a $10 million router order. The aerospace giant had turned to a Silicon Valley start-up called Crescendo Communications for the faster switching technology.

Chambers reportedly asked the Boeing executives what he had to do to get the order. "Start making switches," they said.

In one version of the story, the Boeing people told Chambers point blank that Cisco would have to partner with or buy Crescendo. Around the same time, Ford Motor Company reportedly told Morgridge and Chambers that it, too, was less interested in Cisco's routers than the Crescendo switches. But Cisco was quite narrow-minded on the subject, culturally speaking. As far as the company was concerned, routers were the future of networking, not switches. In fact, Chambers has described Cisco at the time as a router bigot.

Faced with the defection of two major customers, Chambers, Morgridge, and then CTO Ed Kozel put prejudice aside to come up with a strategy, not only for coping with the immediate crisis but also for doing business in such a volatile marketplace going forward. They could never hope to dominate such a market relying solely on internally developed technology. Today it was switches; tomorrow it would be ATM technology—or something else. Things were simply moving too fast. Product-development cycles were dropping below eighteen months, a trend that would continue for years. One answer—perhaps the only answer—was to buy whatever they couldn't develop quickly enough.

And yet the conventional wisdom of the time held that high-tech partnerships and acquisitions simply did not work. Integrating a new organization into the buyer's corporate culture was a time-consuming and tedious process that devoured resources and slowed growth. Acquiring organizations had to assimilate products, people, processes, and culture. And many acquisitions involved layoffs and bad feelings all around.

But whatever convention held to be true, Cisco was confronted by a pressing truth of its own: The company simply did not have the technology its customers were saying they wanted to buy. In the rapidly evolving environment that computer networking had become, Cisco was about to be left behind, a purveyor of yesterday's hardware.

Chambers's experience with outdated products at Wang and IBM heightened his concern over Cisco's aging technology. He was determined to keep apace of the market and believed that innovating through the right acquisition was the solution Cisco needed to remain ahead in its field. Chambers asked Kozel to scout the Valley for likely start-ups with top-notch engineering talent. The strategy was to bring these technologists into the Cisco organization and help them finish their products. Cisco's sales organization and distribution partners would then market the new applications. The tricky part was convincing entrepreneurs that they would be more successful as part of a larger organization.

Among the companies Kozel scouted was, of course, Crescendo. It turned out that Cisco had ties to the Sunnyvale, California-based start-up. The company had received venture money from Don Valentine's Sequoia Capital, and Terry Eger, who with Morgridge had brought Chambers to Cisco, served on the company's board of directors. Chambers approached Cisco's board for permission to buy Crescendo for $100 million in stock. At the time, the board was considering the possibility of merging with either Santa Clara, California-based SynOptics Communications or Cabletron Systems. Both networking operations were about the same size as Cisco, so either deal would have been a merger of equals.

A merger of equals offered some advantages over the acquisition of a start-up. A marriage of the number-one and number-two vendors in a particular market almost always put both enterprises in first place. During periods of fast growth, mergers of equals strengthened management with a fast infusion of high-level people. In such a merger, customer bases were broadened and distribution channels opened.

In Chambers's view, the chief disadvantage of a merger of equals was in the blending of corporate cultures, which he felt was impossible to achieve. In the end, one company's philosophy and focus would have to emerge as the dominant ethos; anything less would leave the combined organizations without a clear leader. He was firm in his conviction that no other factor could compensate for the trouble caused by such a basic incompatibility.

Cisco had worked with both SynOptics and Cabletron on joint projects, so both companies were known entities. According to Chambers, the two firms worked well with Cisco on a few small projects, although some larger undertakings had been less successful. But it was the dramatic difference between the visions held by each of these two companies and the direction in which Chambers was taking Cisco that was the real deal breaker as far as Chambers was concerned. Both SynOptics and Cabletron were technology-driven organizations, evincing the very techno-bigotry that Cisco was trying to outgrow.

Beyond the deliberations over this particular M&A decision, Chambers recalled to Rifkin, lay a distinctly different road ahead for Cisco. With the proposed Crescendo acquisition, he and his colleagues would set out to change the company's organizational structure:

> Our recommendation to the board went like this: Let's go back and build upon our strengths. Let's segment the market much like HP did. Let's break the market into four segments. Let's draw a matrix and adopt a GE mentality and target a 50 percent market share in each area you go into or you don't compete.
>
> Then, we said, let's determine the product, services and distribution needs for each segment and combine the way of getting these products developed and sold—whether internally, through joint development or through acquisition. In essence, we drew a matrix for the board of directors and said, here are the market segments we are going into.[2]

This matrix identified emerging niche markets, from Internet hardware and software to switches and routers, areas in which the company could become a market leader. The only name on that matrix when it was presented to the Cisco board in 1993 was Crescendo's. Over time, the rest of the matrix was filled in with the company's new objectives: to be number one or number two in each market segment in which it competes; to shoot for a 50-percent share in every market; and never to enter a market in which the company could not immediately achieve at least a 20-percent share. To accomplish these goals, Cisco would continue to develop 70 percent of its products internally, but the remaining 30 percent would have to come from acquisitions.

The board approved the acquisition—and for all intents and purposes, the company's new direction. In the fall of that year, Crescendo became the first in a long line of strategic purchases. The deal went smoothly by all accounts, and within a month dozens of Crescendo employees had joined the Cisco ranks.

Switches would never totally replace routers. As the network evolved, the two devices would become complementary technologies. But Chambers had now positioned Cisco to exploit the confluence of those technologies. The company now had the very products that Boeing and Ford had told him they wanted, and the type of technology that customers like AT&T and MCI needed to run their networks.

Reaction to the Crescendo acquisition among industry watchers was overwhelmingly negative. The price tag of $100 million seemed like a lot to pay for a company that had only $10 million in revenues and its first product still on the drawing board. The value of switching technology was anything but certain, and plenty of people thought ATM would outshine it soon enough. To some on Wall Street, it seemed as though Cisco was giving up its frugal ways. Analyst Paul Johnson of First Boston interpreted the deal as a desperation play on Cisco's part and downgraded the company's stock. Other analysts, most of whom perceived the networking marketplace to be especially fickle, did the same, and Cisco's stock dipped for the first time in the company's history.

Yet by July, the end of fiscal 1994, Cisco had earned over $1 billion in annual revenues—double that of the previous year—and had expanded to 2,262 employees. In 1996, the Crescendo group alone produced more than $500 million in annual revenue.

The significance of that first acquisition wouldn't become immediately apparent to the world at large. Chambers and company had bought their way into a market—everyone could see that—but they had also started the process of reinventing their organization, of becoming a one-stop shop in a market that had been considered too technologically complex for any one vendor to dominate. The goal now was to become an end-to-end provider of networking technology.

And something else was happening at Cisco. The company was ramping up to operate in *Internet time,* in which one calendar year equals seven Internet years. Now, instead of focusing on one-year plans, Cisco's people would assess and adjust their tactics on a quarterly basis.

RESISTANCE IS NOT FUTILE

Over the years, Chambers and company refined their acquisitions process into something of a science (reporters loved to call it a "blitzkrieg"). Once a deal had been struck, Cisco mobilized its full-time transition team (reporters loved to call *it* a "SWAT team") to facilitate the integration of the acquired organization. Within months — sometimes weeks — every employee of the acquired company would be integrated. *Every* employee. They would have their new titles, know the names of their new bosses, have all the paperwork on the company health plans and other benefits, and know the URL of the company's internal Web site. Often, Cisco was shipping the acquired company's products under its own label by the time the deal was closed or shortly thereafter.

Cisco's ability to buy the technology it needed and weave it and the assets of the company that spawned it seamlessly into the fabric of the Cisco organization was soon as much a part of the folklore of high tech as the garage millionaire. Performing at its peak, Cisco's M&A machines could acquire and integrate six companies at once. Within two years, the acquisition process had become so much a part of Cisco's culture that everyone, from salespeople to engineers, was attuned to potential deals.

The sheer number of its acquisitions was bound to invite comparisons between Cisco and the Borg, the half-man-half-machine aliens from the *Star Trek* television series who roam the universe assimilating civilizations (especially in a Nerdvana like Silicon Valley, which all but shut down on the day the Star Wars prequel, *The Phantom Menace,* hit local theaters). And that's certainly the way some acquired staffers have seen the company. In a March 2000 article, *Wall Street Journal* reporter Scott Thurm wrote about disgruntled Cerent employees who called Cisco the "Borg of Silicon Valley." Even those who are pleased to find themselves joining the Cisco fold have made the association. During its acquisition, another company happily gave out T-shirts with "We have been assimilated" printed on them.

Cisco has also been compared to a great white shark and to the old Pac-Man video game. Business reporters routinely use verbs like "gobble," "consume," and "digest" to characterize the Cisco acquisitions process. With a nod to Chambers's southern roots, one reporter likened his M&A activities to Sherman storming through Atlanta.

Colorful though these comparisons may be, they don't really work. They miss a key component of the success of Chambers's strategy. The Borg are known for telling their victims "Resistance is futile." But resistance to Cisco *isn't* futile. For all intents and purposes, the company avoids hostile takeovers. To be sure, if Chambers and his acquisitions point men (first Charles Giancarlo, and later, Mike Volpi) wanted something, they went after it, but the approach was more of a courtship than an assault. Time and again, Chambers has declared that he is not interested in buying companies that don't want to be acquired.

He has also enumerated his criteria for a successful merger, a rather conservative blueprint for what was once considered a radical growth plan. According to that blueprint, companies suitable for acquisitions would be fast-growing, focused, entrepreneurial, and culturally similar to Cisco. Generally, they would be small organizations with cutting-edge technology that was ready to pop. Chambers has described the ideal Cisco acquisition as a small start-up that has a great technology product on the drawing board that is going to come out in six to twelve months. And a typical Cisco acquisition was small, a company with between seventy and one hundred employees. Inside the company, firms that fit this description were known as "Cisco Kids."

Geography mattered, too. Cisco would limit itself to three regions: the Silicon Valley near its San Jose headquarters, the Research Triangle in North Carolina, and the Route 128 corridor outside Boston.

Virtually all the transactions have been straight stock swaps, and were until the SEC put the kibosh on such accounting methods, handled as pooling-of-interests transactions. Cisco also invested equity stakes in start-ups aimed at building specific technologies, with carefully tailored options to buy the company outright, which Cisco aimed to exercise when the product shipped.

Chambers is also looking for quick wins for his shareholders and long-term gains for Cisco's employees, customers, and business partners, examining factors that are best described as esoteric: a compatible vision and *chemistry*.

These are hardly the criteria of a Borg-like predator. Chambers is a friendly guy with an affable formula for acquiring and integrating companies—which is not to say that Chambers can't be assertive. Anyone who has been on the receiving end of a Chambers pitch can tell you how determined the persuasive former IBM salesman can be. WorldCom Vice Chairman John Sidgmore recalled for *Washington Post* reporter Mark Leibovitch an incident in which Chambers made a sales pitch that lasted several hours through a 1999 Bruce Springsteen concert at MCI Center. "We were in this suite, and he had me up against a wall," Sidgmore told Leibovitch. "The other people there were sort of freaked out." A Cisco employee who witnessed more than a few Chambers pitches emphasizes his "gentle but relentless" style. "He sort of traps you with those blue eyes," she says. "You really can't help but believe him. I think it's because he believes what he's saying himself."[3]

But "assertive" does not equal "aggressive." Chambers wants to work only with people who want to work with him, and Crescendo fit the bill perfectly. It was geographically close. Its technology and culture were compatible with Cisco's. And its engineers and executives were welcome additions. Crescendo's four cofounders still work for Cisco; the former CEO, Mario Mazzola, is senior vice president of Cisco's enterprise line of business.

In fact, *lots* of the people that Cisco acquired stayed with the company. It's a remarkably underreported value of Chambers's growth-by-acquisitions strategy. Beyond merely adding to the product catalog, Chambers was giving the company access to top engineering talent. In one of the tightest job markets in history, when tech firms were howling about the dearth of qualified people and begging Washington to expand the quota of H-1B visas just so they could tap into a deeper talent pool, Cisco was scooping up engineers and managers by the bucketful.

Larry Bohn, CEO of net.Genesis, has characterized the phenomenon as the No. 1 reason for M&A in the technology industry.[4]

STRATACOM SETS A RECORD

After the Crescendo deal came two more key acquisitions: Ethernet switch maker Kalpana in 1994 and ATM switch maker LightStream a year later. Charles Giancarlo came to Cisco as part of the deal with

Kalpana, a company he cofounded. By the time Chambers had succeeded Morgridge in 1995, the company's M&A machine was well oiled and running smoothly.

In 1996, Cisco added some serious mileage to that machine with its largest acquisition to date—a deal that was, at the time, the largest in the history of the networking industry. Chambers's purchase of high-end switching company StrataCom, Inc., dazzled analysts and made history.

Cisco had worked with its San Jose neighbor on a joint frame-relay forum back in 1989, so StrataCom was a known quantity. The relationship between the companies was friendly, just the way Chambers liked it. Reportedly, less than two weeks after he sat down to dinner with StrataCom CEO Dick Moley to ask if he would be interested in being acquired, the deal was done.

Cisco acquired StrataCom for about $4 billion in shares of Cisco common stock. It was the second-largest acquisition in IT history, after IBM's 1995 purchase of Lotus, and the largest ever in the networking industry. When the deal was completed in late June, Cisco's worldwide workforce swelled from five thousand to about seven thousand. Initially, Moley stayed on at Cisco as a senior vice president and board member, but he left the company in 1997 to become a private investor. (He cofounded Palo Alto-based Storm Ventures.) By combining Cisco's networking technologies with those of StrataCom, Chambers said in a media release issued at the time, "Cisco will become the first vendor to provide advanced network infrastructure for the intranet and Internet environments, and the only vendor to offer end-to-end connectivity across public, private or hybrid networks."

The StrataCom purchase definitely broke Chambers's acquisitions blueprint rule about size. With $500 million in sales and twelve hundred employees, the company was no Cisco Kid. But Chambers had never actually ruled out a big buy, especially if it was the only means available to compete at the level for which he was striving. At the time of the acquisition, Chambers explained to the press that his reasons for baiting his hook for such a big fish was primarily to get up to speed quickly with Ethernet, ATM, and frame-relay technologies. Cisco's breadth of products in these categories was immediately bolstered and expanded by the acquisition, generating almost $800 million.

At the time that Cisco acquired StrataCom, the company was the dominant player in the frame-relay market with a 40-percent share. Analysts expected that market to grow from $800 million in 1995 to about $1.8 billion annually in 1999. And even with a relatively small share of the ATM market (22 percent), the company was still a leader in that segment with revenues of $400 million and an expectation that those revenues would grow to $5 billion by 1999.

Chambers saw the integration of WANs and LANs as a critical trend in networking. Such integration would allow for a connection that spanned the gap between the desktop and the central-office switch. As thin-client proponents like Oracle's CEO Larry Ellison and Sun Microsystems' chief Scott McNealy would soon proclaim, the network was truly becoming the computer.

"StrataCom was the one piece we were missing to be able to play the entire realm," Chambers told *Upside*'s Eric Nee in a 1996 interview. "You could say that customers began to realize the true cost of having five or 10 vendors in their network. How do you troubleshoot across this network if the network has truly become the computer?"[5]

Cisco boasted that it took only ninety days to integrate StrataCom. Later, Chambers amended that claim slightly: "The largest acquisition in terms of dollars that the industry had ever seen is something we integrated into our business in four months." Morgridge, too, commented on the acquisition: "It took a lot longer to assimilate StrataCom, a lot of technology our field force had to learn. They were right next to us and we did a great job in integrating manufacturing, services, purchasing."[6]

But insiders say that StrataCom was a difficult company to assimilate. "It was just too big," one Cisco employee told me. "We had trouble integrating our operating system into StrataCom's switches. It was a real hairball." According to Sanjay Subhedar, StrataCom's former chief financial officer, about a third of StrataCom's sales team left within a few months after losing accounts to Cisco salespeople and because of frustrating changes in their commission plan.

The Cisco-StrataCom deal followed a series of mergers and acquisitions that divided the network-equipment market among a handful of players. Now, Cisco's rivals Bay Networks, 3Com, Cabletron, and Cascade were faced with the daunting task of keeping pace in a market with fewer and fewer acquisitions options.

But Chambers had friends as well as enemies. In 1997, Cisco entered into an alliance with telecom equipment maker Alcatel to provide networking capabilities to telecom and Internet access providers. A year later, it acquired several niche players, including Precept Software, a provider of video-transmission software, and American Internet Corporation, which developed software for set-top boxes and cable modems. Nineteen-ninety-eight was also the year that Cisco's market cap passed the $100 billion mark. Once referred to as the "most invisible major company in high tech," rocketship Cisco was now on everyone's radar.

In 1999 the company made a wireless play by forming a joint venture with Motorola to acquire the fixed wireless assets of Bosch Telecom; the result was high-speed networking services provider Spectra-Point Wireless. Also in 1999, Cisco agreed to collaborate with Qwest Communications on what was expected to become the biggest Internet-based network in the United States.

CERENT BREAKS THE RECORD

By 2000 optical transport—the potentially enormous fiber-optics market from which Cisco had been conspicuously absent—was the new high-speed networking frontier. Optical-networking technology uses light (laser beams) to send bits of information at much faster speeds than conventional electronic-based networks. The Internet boom was driving service providers to optical technologies to widen the Information Highway and unclog their network traffic jams.

Analysts expected the optical transport market to grow to $10 billion by 2002, and Lucent Technologies, Alcatel, and Nortel Networks were already there. Cisco was not. Chandan Sarkar, an analyst at Soundview Financial, has described Cisco as a company with a "hole in the optical transport portion of their portfolio."

Chambers, of course, could see the hole; he could hardly have missed it. During a speech he gave in 1999 at a Dell Computer DirectConnect conference in Austin, Texas, Chambers told his audience, "Anyone who follows our market knows that optical transport was going to explode. This is how the industry is going to evolve. . . . This is going to be a $10 billion-plus market, and if we can execute right, we can get a 20 to 25 percent market share."[7] And, a member of the Cisco M&A team told me, Chambers was "gunning for Lucent."

Although the company's fiber-optic expertise was nominal, Cisco did own 9 percent of a hot fiber-optics start-up: Petaluma, California-based Cerent Corporation. Cisco had purchased a stake in the start-up fiber-optics equipment maker in 1998.

Exactly how the Cerent deal came down depends on whom you talk to. In one version of the story, Chambers got to know Cerent CEO Carl Russo when they met at a conference near Laguna Beach, California, in May 1999. "I don't think I can afford to buy you guys," Chambers reportedly said to Russo. "I don't think you can afford not to," Russo replied. But in another version of the story, Russo wasn't so sure he wanted to be assimilated. Chambers asked him what it would cost to buy his company, to which a former Cerent employee told me Russo answered, "How much would it cost for you to leave us alone?" After all, Russo was CEO of a cutting-edge start-up, and he was putting together an initial public offering (IPO) he was hoping to implement in the fall, and his employees were expecting to get rich. An IPO was the brass ring in Silicon Valley, and every employee of every start-up knew it. An acquisition, on the other hand, could destroy their dreams of instant wealth and send them scuttling to Monster.com in search of employment.

But Chambers and Mike Volpi were now hot on Russo's trail. They had a hole to plug, and Cerent seemed like the perfect peg. Its hundred-member sales team was a big one for a start-up. Chambers liked the emphasis, and its crowded headquarters was even plainer than Cisco's. Russo's "office" was an eight-foot-by-eight-foot cubicle.

During an August meeting in the United Airlines Red Carpet Club at San Francisco International Airport, Volpi reportedly offered Russo $4 billion for his company—as much as Cisco had paid for StrataCom, its largest acquisition. Russo countered with $6.9 billion. "It was a ballsy move on Russo's part," a former Cerent employee told me. "We had only made about $10 million during the entire life of the company." At a meeting two days later at Cisco headquarters in San Jose, California, Chambers made Russo an offer he couldn't refuse: 100 million shares of stock, then valued at about $6.3 billion, for the 91 percent of Cerent that Cisco didn't already own.

When Cerent employees gathered in a hotel ballroom on August 25, most were anticipating big news about the company's upcoming IPO. But rumors were circulating. Some curious workers on the company loading dock had opened a carton full of coffee mugs. The mugs were emblazoned with the Cisco logo and the message "Welcome to the Team."

The initial reaction to Russo's revelation that Cerent was being assimilated was shock and more than a little outrage. (These were the folks who compared Cisco to the Borg, remember.) But the shock wore off as soon as he announced the sale price: 1.445 Cisco shares for each Cerent share. At $66.375 (Cisco's previous day's closing price), each Cerent share was now worth about $96. Lots of people were going to get rich after all.

Cisco acquisitions were never about layoffs. In fact, many Cisco Kids hit the jackpot, and word was getting around about the potential profitability of being acquired by the company. Another member of the Cisco M&A team recalled the day they assembled the employees of Pipelinks to explain the effect of that acquisition on their stock: "We were there to explain the process of exchanging their shares with Cisco shares. People kept raising their hands, asking us how long the process would take. Could we write them a letter saying how many shares they were going to get and how much they would be worth? Everyone in the room was focused on the money. As a joke, I asked them how many were planning to buy a house. Hands shot up all over the room."

Russo would stay on as vice president of Cisco's new optical-networking group. In addition to that record-setting sale price, Russo exacted several concessions from Chambers and company, the most striking of which was Cisco's agreement that Russo would have final say over layoffs of his former employees. No Cerent employee could be fired or significantly reassigned without his approval. Ever. It was an odd stipulation, and perhaps an odder concession. Cisco had long maintained a policy of keeping all acquired employees for a year, but with so many Cerent people coming from the telecom industry, where "acquisition" equaled "layoff," Russo believed it was the only way to handle the merger. Only a handful of Cerent's approximately 400 employees left after the acquisition.

The Cerent purchase marked the beginning of a rush into optical networking. Hot on the heels of its biggest merger yet, Cisco bought Monterey Networks, Pirelli Optical Systems, and Qeyton Systems. Add the Cerent deal to the equation, and Cisco spent about $12 billion to assemble a suite of optical products to offer the big telecoms.

Cisco's acquisition strategy had shifted the company from an engineering-driven enterprise to a sales-driven concern. Chambers would talk about Cisco doing "small-R-big-D": in other words, the company would eventually find itself spending its time and money improving its own products and making acquired products work with the existing product line. Cisco would spend far less on R&D than a company like IBM or Lucent. At Cisco, only about 14 percent of the company's budget was earmarked for research and development. That's around $3 billion annually, give or take.

By early 2001, about 40 percent of Cisco's $19 billion in annual revenues were coming from acquisitions. Chambers the salesman, the listener, the talker, the technologically agnostic nonengineer, was winning market share and accolades. And if there's one thing Chambers loves, it's winning.

In the end, Chambers's acquisition strategy might be seen as something very personal, an expression of a lesson the man learned in childhood. The bright boy who couldn't read found the solution to his problem outside himself, in the knowledge and insights of his teacher, Kitty Walter. Before Chambers arrived in Silicon Valley, companies that looked outside for technology solutions were viewed as weak. Many tech-industry mavens still see things that way. But Chambers the agnostic saw nothing weak in that approach. As Cisco's then-CTO Judy Estrin put it back in 1998, "John has instilled a culture in which it's not a sign of weakness but a sign of strength to say, 'I can't do everything myself. I will find a partner and trust myself to be able to manage the process.'"[8]

NOTES

1. Glenn Rifkin, "Growth By Acquisition: The Case of Cisco Systems," *Strategy + Business,* Q2, 1997.
2. Ibid.
3. Mark Leibovitch, "A Rain God Confronts a Harsh Climate: CEO's Optimism Tested by Downturn," *Washington Post,* April 6, 2001.
4. Andy Serwer, "There's Something About Cisco," *Fortune,* May 2000.
5. Eric Nee, "Interview with John Chambers of Cisco Systems, Inc." *Upside,* July 1, 1996.
6. Glenn Rifkin, "Growth By Acquisition: The Case of Cisco Systems," *Strategy + Business,* Q2, 1997.
7. Sandeep Junnarkar, "Cisco Buys Cerent, Monterey Networks," CNET News.com, August 26, 1999.
8. Andrew Kupfer, "The Real King of the Internet," *Fortune,* September 1998.

CHAPTER 8

THE CISCO SEDUCTION

For most of his tenure at Cisco Systems, John Chambers has presided over an accelerating rate of company growth. To maintain those record-setting growth rates, Chambers has had to increase his workforce at a similarly high rate. In each quarter of 1996, the company hired more than one thousand new employees, making it responsible for about 10 percent of the total net job gains in Silicon Valley. At its peak, just before the economic downturn forced Chambers to lay people off in the spring of 2000, Cisco Systems employed approximately forty thousand people.

Along the way, Chambers created a corporate culture that attracts and keeps the best and the brightest. Benefits like telecommuting options and support for continuing education help to lure top people. The company built its own day-care center, complete with technology that allows parents to monitor their children from their desktops via Webcams. The idea, as human resources director Barbara Beck told me in early 2000, when the company was breaking ground on its new child-care center in Milpitas, California, is to help employees "move seamlessly between on-the-job and off-the-job duties throughout the day." Toward that end, Cisco has also installed high-speed DSL lines in employees' homes in order to facilitate productivity and support alternative working arrangements. It was perks like these that caused *Fortune* magazine to put Cisco Systems near the top of its list of "The 100 Greatest Companies to Work for in the US" three years in a row.

And the boss is no slouch as a recruiter. The TV news magazine "20/20" called John Chambers America's Number-one Boss and showed him handing out ice cream to his employees with his trademark smile. What could be a better recruiting tool than that?

Maybe the money, among other things. Cisco was, until recently, a great place to get rich. At its peak, Cisco's stock was a compelling recruiting tool. In the ten years after the company's initial public offering, its stock split eight times and rose about 8,000 percent. Shares bought back in 1990 for the $18 initial asking price were worth $14,000 in 2000. By 2000, Cisco had made at least 2,500 of its 23,000 employees stock-option millionaires.

Put it all together and you have what one former Cisco employee called the "Cisco seduction."

TIGHT TECH

Nowhere has the market for good people been tighter than in the tech sector. In fact, until the economic downturn, Cisco was competing for people in one of the tightest job markets in history. The tech sector in particular was a seller's market. What employers were willing to do in that job market to attract and keep good people was nothing short of amazing. In Silicon Valley, where the job market was as hot as it gets and showed no signs of cooling, local employers were bending over backward to lure the best and brightest to their companies. From on-site dental services to get-your-head-together, paid sabbaticals; from concierge programs to special on-site private nursing rooms for new moms, companies in the area were offering perks and amenities unheard of just a few years ago. Need your car washed? No problem, the company will hire a service to wash your vehicle out in the parking lot. No time to drop off and pick up your dry cleaning? No worries, the company will have it picked up at the office and delivered back to you. No effort was spared to make employees happy and to keep them productive and focused on the work at hand.

In Silicon Valley, ground zero for the New Economy, the notion that employees were valuable assets was nothing new. It was Bill Hewlett and Dave Packard who started this particular ball rolling back in the 1950s. As their garage-born company began to prosper, they instituted a policy that has come to be known as The H-P Way. Bill Hewlett has summed up his company's celebrated code of benevolent values this way: "I feel that in general terms it is the policies and actions that flow from the belief that men and women want to do a good job, a creative job, and that if they are provided the proper environment they will do so."

And the notion was certainly not new at Cisco. In fact, Chambers has said that he modeled much of his company's corporate culture after H-P. Simply put, he tried to foster a value-centered management approach, focused on teamwork and respect for people, that made his shareholders profits, and his company a place where people wanted to do good work.

Chambers's approach seems to fit a new mold for high-tech executives. The very technology he promotes—the network—speeds up the pace at which people can interact, enabling (and maybe even forcing) a more collaborative environment. The explosion of information access in the workplace is obliging managers to be more candid and more genuine, if for no other reason than they simply can no longer hide from the rank and file.

Dr. Robert Rosen, CEO of the consulting firm Healthy Companies International, in Washington, D.C., has observed that information technology is creating an environment in which everyone has access to information, and that this expanded access is changing power dynamics within organizations, particularly high-tech companies where, as Rosen explains, "people have different kinds of psychological mind-sets, so they have to be managed very differently." Rosen sees the management of such employees as a challenging task, and he has singled out John Chambers as an example of a high-tech executive who is meeting that challenge successfully.[1]

For his part, Chambers seems to have a clear understanding of his role and what it takes to manage people in this new environment. "If you take my top 100 managers in Cisco," he said in an interview, "I know what motivates most all of them and I know what's important to them. We try to align the goals of the company with the goals of the individual and make that work all the way through our organization. I've practiced it at the top so that it should cascade all the way through the company."[2]

SHOW ME THE MONEY

But no one works for free. Money matters, and in Silicon Valley money matters more. It was and still is an expensive place to live. The economy may have cooled, but it was hot throughout the 1990s, and the local living expenses it warmed up are still smoldering. Over the last decade of the twentieth century, local housing prices went through the stratosphere. Sky-high living expenses meant that local employers like Cisco, simply had to pay top dollar to its people. The average salary in Silicon Valley was nearly $50,000 in 1998, compared to the national average of $30,000.

In the late 1990s during its biggest growth spurt, Cisco was competing for top talent with sizzling dotcoms that had a particular type of currency that Cisco lacked: pre-public company stock options. With venture-capital money flowing like espresso at a Starbuck's, why work for a big company when you can hook up with some twenty-somethings in a San Francisco loft and ride the start-up train. It wasn't always about your employees' paychecks; it was about what they could make on your stock.

And, as it turned out, it was a lot like playing the lottery. Tech heads from all over the country were coming to Silicon Valley to get in on the ground floor of promising start-ups, and it was tough to compete with such a stirring promise of wealth, especially in the market for younger employees with no kids or mortgage and a youthful willingness to accept a much greater level of risk to make their fortunes or "to get the money thing out of the way," as one T-shirt millionaire once told me.

But then again, at Cisco, top talent didn't need to roll the dice to reap the benefits of the hot economy. Hell, Cisco was practically a sure thing. By the beginning of 2000, it was a millionaire-making machine.

ACQUIRED TALENT

Cisco's acquisition engine is best-known for powering the company's growth, and for giving it a kind of instant R&D to cope with rapidly evolving technologies, changing markets, and shifting customer demands. But, as I pointed out in the previous chapter, one of the greatest strengths of Cisco's M&A strategy was the access it provided to skilled people. The tech sector had been a seller's job market for years, but Chambers and company staffed their growing enterprise to bursting with the relentless and accelerating pace of their acquisitions.

Start-up companies, whose employees might typically prefer to wait for the IPO cash-out, were beginning to view a Cisco acquisition as an alternative exit strategy. In an acquisition, options for unregistered and restricted private company stock would be swapped for options to acquire Cisco's gold currency stock. One Cisco insider told me a story about being in the room during an informational meeting with employees of a soon-to-be-acquired company. Members of Cisco's integration team and lawyers from the company's outside legal team were there to answer questions about how the acquired employees' stock and options would be exchanged for Cisco stock and options. Many of the employees from the new company were anxious to learn how quickly the exchange would occur and whether employees could obtain some formal advance notice of the number of shares or options they'd be receiving. One of the lawyers conducting the meeting asked, "Just out of curiosity, how many of you here are planning on buying a house with your proceeds from this acquisition?" Hands shot up all over the room. "It was clear to all of us," the source said, "that the majority of these folks were about to make some very serious money."

Chambers has often said that he is not in the business of acquiring technologies but of acquiring people. In a 1997 interview, he talked about that idea with Glenn Rifkin:

> [Cisco] is different from the automotive or financial industries, where you are acquiring process, customer base and distribution. So when we acquire something, we are not acquiring distribution capabilities or manufacturing expertise. We—Cisco—are very good at that. We are acquiring technology. In this business, if you are acquiring technology, you are acquiring people.
>
> And if you don't keep those people, you have made a terrible, terrible investment. We pay between $500,000 and $2 million per person in an acquisition, which is a lot. So you can understand that if you don't keep the people, you've done a tremendous disservice to your shareholders and customers. So we focus first on the people and how we incorporate them into our company, and then we focus on how to drive the business.[3]

Chambers has also said that he judges the success of an acquisition by how many of the people from the acquired company he keeps. For years, his record in that regard was remarkable. At one point, the company's attrition rate among acquired employees was lower than the rate for staff hired directly—and attrition rates for those workers was among the lowest in the computer industry. In a market in which attrition rates of 30 percent were not uncommon, Cisco's overall attrition rate of less than 5 percent was positively miraculous.

The company has kept a remarkable number of executives from its acquisitions. Its goal was always to keep the top exec in an acquisition because keeping the boss made it more likely that Cisco would keep the rank and file. One of the reasons Chambers has managed to hold on to so much top talent—besides the money—is that he gives acquired executives a chance to play a major role in the merged organization.

Probably the company's most famous personnel acquisition was Andreas (Andy) Bechtolsheim, originally one of the cofounders of Sun Microsystems. Sun had grown into a $7-billion-a-year company by 1995, when Andy Bechtolsheim left to start Granite Systems. When he approached Chambers to license some of Cisco's software, the two struck a bargain for an acquisition instead. Cisco acquired the Gigabit Ethernet start-up a year later for $220 million. To everyone's surprise—everyone outside of the two companies, at least—Bechtolsheim stayed on at Cisco as vice president. He liked Cisco's small-company mentality. A year after he joined the company, he told *Wired* magazine, "So many of us have come from companies Cisco acquired that when we introduce ourselves, we usually add where we were last." And he liked Chambers. "You couldn't genetically engineer a better leader."[4]

Legendary high-tech entrepreneur Judith Estrin was another Cisco acquisition. Estrin joined Cisco in 1998, when her multimedia networking company, Precept Software, was acquired. She had founded the company with her husband, Bill Carrico, who also joined Cisco as a senior vice president. As CTO, Estrin helped to drive Cisco's integrated voice and data efforts. Estrin left the company two years later to start a new venture with her husband. It would be their fifth project together. Acquisitions master Mike Volpi stepped into her shoes but retained his title as chief strategy officer.

Charles Giancarlo came to Cisco as part of the 1994 acquisition of Kalpana, a company he cofounded. Chambers offered him the job of running Cisco's business development organization, in which capacity he would spearhead acquisitions. The idea was to put someone in that role who had been through the process. Giancarlo now sits on Cisco's executive board.

And there are other examples: Mario Mazzola, cofounder and CEO of Crescendo, joined Cisco when it acquired his company in 1993. He became senior vice president of the company's enterprise line of business. Carl Russo, who was the CEO of Cerent, became vice president for Cisco's optical-networking group with the acquisition of that company.

SEEKING THE SEEKERS

But it was never just the fish netted in acquisitions that stocked the company's brimming work pool. By the mid-1990s, Cisco was also a highly sought-after employer, widely known for its exciting work environment and its respect for its employees. Cisco has been just as competitive when it comes to hiring as the company has been in the product and service markets it dominates.

In its pursuit of so-called passive job seekers, which is what Cisco calls people who already have good jobs and don't yet know that they ought to be working at Cisco, the company has been known to set up focus groups with senior engineers and marketing executives from competing companies — the very people it wants to hire — to find out about them and figure out how to lure them to the company. Recruiters ask focus group members about their jobs, how they spend their free time, what Web sites they visit, and how they feel about job hunting. And then they show up at art fairs and microbrewery festivals and hand out business cards. According to one company insider, Cisco recruiters especially like Silicon Valley's annual home and garden show, which tends to attract young, successful, first-time homebuyers. If they can afford a home in the Valley, the thinking goes, they're probably top talent, and Cisco wants them.

In the style of a true New Economy company, Cisco has also turned the Web into a recruitment tool. Active job seekers who might fit in at Cisco are typically Net-savvy candidates from around the world. Not only are they likely to prefer looking for job posting on a Web site, but Cisco can reach thousands of them worldwide with hundreds of jobs listing for pennies.

Even more innovative was the company's so-called "friend" program. In response to its focus group studies in 1998, the company launched an initiative to help prospects meet someone at Cisco who could describe what it's like to work there. The program matched Cisco employees through a Web page with potential hires who had similar backgrounds and skills. These "friends" would call the prospects to tell them in their own words about life at the company. Becoming a friend was entirely voluntary, but Cisco made it worthwhile, financially. The company offered its employees a hefty referral fee, which started at around $500, and a lottery ticket for a free trip to Hawaii. Approximately a thousand employees signed up.

CANDYMAN

It's almost impossible for the CEO of a company with 40,000 employees to keep in touch with the rank and file, but Chambers tries harder than most chief executives. Regularly, he cruises the hallways of Cisco City, chatting with employees and handing out ice cream and candy.

"If you ran into John Chambers in the elevator," a former employee told me, "he would throw a question at you. 'What can we do better?' 'What do you think about this part of the culture?' When he asks that stuff, he really wants to know."

Once a month, Chambers hosts a breakfast in the company cafeteria open to any employee whose birthday falls in that month. They call it the Birthday Bunch, and few miss a chance for the closest thing to a one-on-one with the boss they are ever likely to get. The meetings are unscripted, and employees are free to ask Chambers anything they want. According to more than one employee, he answers any question they ask him. In more than a few cases, they say, his answers are more honest than his managers'. "No presentation," a former employee recalls. "He would sit up there with a couple of Diet Cokes and answer any question he was asked."

Chambers is enormously popular among his employees. Even after the layoffs of 2001, few current or former Cisco-ites would say much to criticize the CEO—at least not him personally. And it's not just a few ice cream sandwiches or the occasional let's-just-chat breakfast that has endeared him to his people. It is most likely his attitude toward leadership and his emphasis on teamwork that has won them over. Chambers has often compared the CEO's job to the role of the lead dog on a dogsled. He never thinks of himself as the guy on the sled with the whip.

When Chambers talks about what he looks for in his managers, he reveals another reason his people tend to be so loyal. He talks about esoteric qualities like "vision" and "instinct." But he's primarily interested in a more concrete quality: the ability to develop a team. He cares about trust and integrity, industry knowledge and communication skills. And, of course, he wants them to be customer-focused. But he looks for all of these things only in the context of *teamwork.*

Whatever the cause, the admiration Chambers commands at Cisco is palpable. And even after his golden-boy image was tarnished by his economic reversals in 2001, he continued to hold their esteem. Fund manager James Cramer once said of Chambers's popularity with his employees, "I've never seen a group of people worship a guy like that. They'd walk through fire for him."[5]

"He's the most positive person in the world," one employee told me. "And when he sees that something isn't working, he changes it." "The man is a visionary," another employee explained. "He surrounds himself with great people. And he listens to people. It's not unheard of for an employee to get so fed up and send an e-mail directly to John Chambers. And they don't get hammered by John for doing that. He looks into it."

STRETCHING AND EMPOWERING

Once you get past the compensation packages and the corporate culture, and even the popular boss, there's the work. Whatever they're paying, whatever the perks, at some point employers have to present a compelling job. In Silicon Valley, in particular, the work itself matters.

"I think [our biggest attractor] is the excitement of working at a cutting-edge company," Cisco spokesperson Steve Langdon told me in a 2000 interview. "This is a place where you are empowered to make a difference. If you've got an idea, you can pursue it."

During his early years at IBM, Chambers felt held back by a corporate culture that encouraged its people to stick to conservative, makeable goals, to avoid the uncertainty that goes with pushing into unknown territory. His experience at IBM with the manager who criticized him for setting ten goals, nine of which he met and one of which he missed, stayed with him. Better to set three goals and meet them all, his boss had told him. His manager had failed to grasp the value of reaching beyond your known capabilities. It was always one of his chief complaints about his time at the company. He wouldn't make that mistake at Cisco. So it's not surprising to find at the center of Cisco's corporate culture the concept of "stretch goals."

If there is a management concept at Cisco that can be said to be quintessential Chambers, it is stretch goals, and they are a big piece of the Cisco culture. The idea is simple: Managers help their people at Cisco to set goals that they can meet, but at the same time they set goals that are . . . well . . . a *stretch*—something they very well might not make. If the goal is to complete a project in a month, the stretch goal might be to complete it in three weeks. If the employee makes the goal, great; if he doesn't, no penalty. And more often than not, he or she achieves part of the stretch goal and improves on the actual goal in the process. What stretch goals accomplish, their proponents say, is to get people taking risks and thinking outside the box.

Chambers determined that a traditional, top-down corporate hierarchy wasn't a suitable organizational structure for a company promoting stretch goals. Consequently, to support this kind of approach, Chambers and his executive staff set about restructuring the company from an organization dependent on a very tight central management group with the top four or five people making all the decisions to the empowerment of groups. The idea was to empower people and then hold them accountable for their results; not in a sink-or-swim kind of way, but rather with support and guidance to keep them from making wrong turns.

The empowerment idea, as implemented at Cisco, had effects that went way beyond stretch goals. It also gave employees the power to act without getting endless permissions. If an employee saw something that needed doing, and he or she could make the case for it, they were free to get it done. The upside of empowerment the Cisco way was that it could nurture an organization that would not get bogged down in bureaucracy, an evil the cost of which Chambers had seen personally.

But there was a downside to the policy. As one employee put it, "They empower you, absolutely. But if something goes wrong, you are also empowered to take the fall. It sounds good, but you end up spending a lot of your time covering your ass."

Another problem was the very corporate structure that Chambers implemented to facilitate empowerment. There were lots of overlaps among business units, especially with all the acquisitions. "Whatever you did often affected lots of other people," one ex-employee explained. "You didn't have to go up the ladder for approval, but you had to go across the organization to make sure that you were in lock step with everybody else. The upshot was, you spent your life in meetings, making sure that what you were empowered to do was okay with somebody else, justifying why you were doing it this way, and making sure that you hadn't ruffled any feathers or that you weren't inadvertently getting someone else in trouble."

DILUTING AND DISTORTING

Chambers is known for asking employees he passes in the hallways at Cisco City, "Are you having fun today?" For many Cisco employees, the honest answer to that question in recent years would have to be "no." Some former employees call the place a "meat grinder." The culprit, they say, isn't Chambers, whom even the most disgruntled ex-Cisco-ites are loath to criticize, but a distortion of his principles.

The way in which the stretch-goals concept has been implemented is a case in point, they say. Cisco City is a highly competitive environment full of Type A personalities. According to some insiders, more than a few of the company's managers have turned what ought to be stretches into the goals themselves. In those situations, the stretch became some utterly unrealistic objective that employees found demoralizing. Others have suggested that, with the acquisitions spree of 1999 and 2000, in which Cisco added a phenomenal number of people to its organization, key components of the corporate culture were simply diluted by the inflow of bodies.

"The longer I was there," one former employee told me, "the more the place came to look like a duck. On the surface, the duck is gliding along the water, but underneath, he's paddling like hell. I think John Chambers is a phenomenal human being, really, but I'm afraid that there's a disconnect, that he doesn't always know how the things he starts get finished out in the company."

In at least one case, an employee took his empowerment too far. In April of 2001, the month in which Cisco's stock hit a two-year low and just before the company would announce a massive layoff, Bob Gordon, a Vice-President of business development, was arrested and accused of embezzling more than $10 million in schemes related to Cisco's investments in two smaller technology companies.

In what the *San Jose Mercury News* called at the time an "egregious example of buzzword abuse," Gordon reportedly told a Cisco security manager that the money shuffles were merely evidence of "thinking outside the box."

FRUGAL BUT NOT CHEAP

Frugality is another fundamental component of the Cisco corporate culture. This one was handed down from John Morgridge—the man who handed Chambers a discount airport parking pass after he turned in his first expense account. Chambers and all top executives fly coach, unless they pay for their own upgrade. No one has an unlimited expense account. No one has a reserved parking space on the company's San Jose campus. All employees share hotel rooms at events. Cisco City is a nicely landscaped but spare campus, and inside everyone, including Chambers, works out of twelve-foot-by-twelve-foot offices. No executive washrooms here.

The walls of the company cafeteria and break rooms are hung with frugality tips, reminding employees that using a partner airline saves an average of $100 per ticket and that booking conferences at Cisco conference centers is cheaper than booking them in hotels. And recycling bins are everywhere.

The idea is not to pinch pennies unnecessarily, but to run a lean, efficient company. A Cisco employee described the concept as "frugal, not cheap." For example, Cisco standardizes its hardware and software ruthlessly. Basically, the company uses one brand of PC, one kind of database, one brand of server—all good products, but cheaper to buy in bulk and to maintain.

At least that's the way it's supposed to work. Employees report that directors don't always share hotel rooms, and of course Chambers now has his own jet. To Diane Sawyer's question, posed during Chambers's 2000 interview for "20/20," "Is there a company plane?" he answered "Absolutely not." He reportedly bought the plane shortly after the interview.

To keep everybody focused on the company's vision, Cisco employees carry the company's cultural imperatives with them on their ID badges. Actually, they carry three badges: one is the security ID badge, with the employee's name and photo; one has the company's mission and basic values printed on one side, with additional principles that management wants to emphasize for the coming year on the other side; and a third badge carries the company's goals for the year. The culture badges are printed with buzzwords like "Interoperability," which proclaims the company's technological agnosticism, and "Frugality," which touts the company's frugal-but-not-cheap philosophy, and "Help Us to Conform to ISO 9001 Standards," which speaks for itself.

For the most part, Cisco's people seem to accept the company's cultural imperatives. The environment doesn't work for everyone, and lapses and inconsistencies are probably inevitable, but in the main, it seems to work.

One employee, who said that she was very skeptical about the culture badges and the company's incessant sloganeering when she first went to work at Cisco, told me a story about an event that brought her around:

"My second week there we had a team offsite of sixty people who went up to Redwood City to help mud and tape a Habitat for Humanity house. Instead of going out and boozing it up, or playing on a ropes course. We were all working together for a common good."

NOTES

1. Colleen O'Connor, "High Touch for High Tech," *Business 2.0,* February 2000.
2. Ibid.
3. Glenn Rifkin, "Growth By Acquisition: The Case of Cisco Systems," *Strategy + Business,* Q2, 1997.
4. Kathleen Weigner, "Gigabit Ethernet," *Wired,* March 1997.
5. Joshua Cooper Ramo, "Cisco Guards the Gates." *TIME,* June 9, 1997.

CHAPTER 9

E-VANGELIST

Few high-tech executives can match John Chambers when it comes to evangelizing the new Internet economy—before, during, and even after the dot-com bust. Beginning in 1997, when the company began to emerge from tech obscurity, Chambers stepped into the public spotlight to represent a company that was changing the "way people live, work, play, and learn." It was a catch phrase, to be sure, but when you heard Chambers say it, you wanted to believe it, partly because you knew he *meant* it, but also because he might be right.

Chambers stepped into that spotlight armed with an ironclad belief that we were in the midst of a revolution, that the Internet was changing everything, and that Cisco was in the "sweet spot," where technology touches and transforms not only business, but all of life. The Industrial Revolution had brought people together with machines in factories, he said, but this new Internet Revolution was bringing people together with information in cyberspace. And people were now competing in a global marketplace. This new revolution would have as great an impact on society as the old one, and it would happen in a handful of years, not decades.

In fact, by 1997 we were already well into the "fourth technology era." And the central enabling technology of this new era was *internetworking*. In this emerging network-centric marketplace, the demands of competition would be very different. Quickness and nimbleness would be everything. The fast would beat the slow in this brave new world, and the companies that survived into the Internet Century would do so not because of their size, their geographic locations, or their physical assets, but because of their agility.

Chambers brought something new to the technology CEO's bully pulpit. When he spoke, it wasn't as a techier-than-thou computer maven, letting his barely computer-literate brethren in on the secret of The Next Big Thing. His was an everyman message, delivered not by an engineer wearing a CEO's hat, but by a businessman using the network to solve problems and make money.

The more Chambers spoke, the more people listened. Soon, his warnings at conferences that fellow execs should get on the Net if they hoped to survive the next technology era were taken as prophetic. In 1997, a *Time* magazine reporter was moved to observe that Chambers "attracts more groupies at trade shows than the Spice Girls on a London street."[1]

And his audience grew almost as fast as his company. He gave hundreds of speeches. He appeared at trade shows and conferences all over the world. Never mind that he wasn't an engineer. In fact, thank god he wasn't. Here was a technology CEO we could all understand. Reporters described him often as straight-talking and affable.

That his talk was delivered with southern inflections served mainly to distinguish him from his tech-touting brethren. His accent wasn't actually a twang, as so many reporters have described it. He spoke, rather, in courtly cadences that *Fortune* writer Andy Serwer once described as a "gentle Piedmont" instead of the "pinched Appalachian you might expect."[2] And his growing audience responded to his blond good looks (not *too* good, with that receding hairline, which just made him more human), his enthusiastic talk about teamwork and empowerment, and his relentless optimism about the new technology era.

Here was a CEO who *got it* without looking down his nose at those who were still struggling to make sense of a world in flux. His message was straightforward and consistent: Companies that missed technology changes, left business models in place that needed changing, and failed to use the technology and the applications themselves were going to be left behind.

And was he confident. He believed that Cisco would one day be to the networking industry what Microsoft has been to the software industry, and he shared that belief with anyone who would listen. He also believed that Cisco was in a position to impact society in world-changing ways. "We are truly empowering the Internet generation as we move into the Internet century," Chambers told *Business Week.* "We have the chance to become one of the most influential companies in history."[3]

INDUSTRY SPOKESMAN

Chambers took on the role of industry spokesman somewhat reluctantly. His predecessor, John Morgridge, had kept a low profile. Routers weren't the glamorous user-facing products that PCs, workstations, and cutting-edge software were. Cisco's products were invisible to users, and for a long time so was the company.

Even as recently as 1996, Cisco Systems was one of the least visible companies in high tech. Cisco dominated computer networking and had a market cap of $25 billion, but neither the company nor its CEO were particularly well known. In fact, no one outside the technology business community and its Silicon Valley neighborhood knew much about the company. The business press had noticed Cisco's acquisition activity—six acquisitions since John Chambers had become CEO a year earlier. And the record-setting StrataCom deal was hard to ignore. But by and large, Cisco was on very few radar screens.

Chambers has said that his relative anonymity in those days was the result of a conscious effort. Both he and his former boss, John Morgridge, had deliberately stayed out of the spotlight. "Neither John Morgridge nor I had a particular desire to be real visible," Chambers said in a 1996 interview. "It wasn't one of the things that motivated us."[4]

But the company was moving away from so-called direct-touch sales, which demanded face time with decision makers in large organizations. As the company began utilizing indirect sales channels, and as it began reaching out to medium and small customers, company visibility began to matter. Those kinds of customers bought brand names, and Cisco was still being confused with a hotel food supplier.

Chambers has said that, although he was reconciled to the fact that what sells in this industry is a leader you can talk to and interview, he didn't like the idea of taking on a more public role. He would rather spend his time with customers than reporters, but he didn't see that he had much choice. "You can have the best products, the best service organization in the world, the best strategy, but if the products are being consumed indirectly and the people who are asking for the vendor selection don't know that, they aren't going to ask for Cisco," he told *Upside* magazine in 1996. "So it's something we're going to have to do more of that isn't particularly one of my top enjoyable things to do."[5]

Of course, Chambers is nothing if not a team player. If an industry spokesman was what his company needed, an industry spokesman is what it would get. Who better to take on that role, at least from Cisco's point of view, than networking's ultimate salesman?

MAN WITH A MESSAGE

In 1997, Chambers got a preview of things to come when he agreed to speak at a CEO retreat in Napa Valley, California. He wondered why they would want someone to talk Internet plumbing at dinner. He ended up speaking for an hour and a half—longer than he'd planned—and to his surprise, his audience was never bored.

By 1999, Chambers was spending more and more of his time focused on high-visibility activities. He has accepted the role and pursued it earnestly. "Evangelizing? I spend way more than half my time on that," Chambers told *Fortune* in 1999. "You've got to evangelize the concept."[6]

The company viewed his activities in this vein as cost effective. "One of the least expensive ways to use your CEO is as an elevated spokesman," chairman John Morgridge once remarked.[7] And Chambers got some great reviews from his own people. Don Valentine, the venture capitalist who provided the original financing for the company and later served as its first chairman, has said that Chambers's appearances "have ulterior motives, and they're to advance the cause of the company, not John Chambers. . . . I think John, given his preferences, would just like to visit customers."[8]

Chambers is often likened to a preacher, probably because he is southern and because the industry term for a great deal of what he does nowadays—promoting the core concepts of cutting-edge technologies—is "evangelizing." He is an evangelist, but if you watch him—really watch him—prowling the stage during a trade-show keynote, speaking at a Commonwealth Club luncheon, or sitting down with a television interviewer, you won't see a preacher. His tempo and meter are markedly pedagogic. He speaks in rapid-fire sentences, and he queries his audience like a college professor. Watch him closely, and you'll see that he's *explaining* things. He's selling, of course, always selling, but this man isn't preaching, he's *teaching*.

In a 1999 press release, Chambers said, "The Internet will reshape virtually everything from personal communications to the balance of power between companies as well as countries. The Internet revolution will determine which companies survive and which get left behind. Increasingly, the Internet is recognized as the key driver in our global economy."

Teacher or preacher, that was his basic message, and he hammered it home whenever he could. *The Internet is changing the way we work, live, play, and learn;* it was no longer a bold statement, but when Chambers began to shout it from the rooftops, it was still somewhat radical. IT was still an expense item, not a source of productivity gains. Oracle's CEO, Larry Ellison, and Sun Microsystems' chief, Scott McNealy, had been saying that the network was the computer, describing this period as the "post-PC era," and talking about "thin clients." But that was just tech talk. Chambers was talking about doing business.

THE TUBE

In 1998, the company's market cap surpassed $100 billion. Cisco had done in twelve years what it had taken Microsoft twenty years to accomplish. Maybe Chambers wasn't just blowing smoke when he talked about becoming the next Microsoft.

As the press finally took notice of the company's warp-speed growth, the man in the cockpit of "Rocketship Cisco" got his share of good press. He was Mr. Internet, the Next Jack Welch, the Best Boss in America, and the High Priest of Good Management.

Now the company was ready to take the wraps off in earnest. After a decade of virtually no advertising, Cisco launched its first TV ad campaign in August 1998. The notoriously frugal company budgeted $40 million for the twelve-month campaign in the United States and $20 million overseas.

The ads were state-of-the-art, polished, and professionally produced. They featured a succession of children, adults, and seniors reciting facts about the Internet. And the tag line was memorable: "Virtually all Internet traffic travels along the systems of one company . . . Cisco Systems. Empowering the Internet generation." The TV ads didn't exactly make Cisco a household name, but the company was no longer enjoying its comfortable obscurity. Chambers and company were positioning Cisco as a communications company, something the public could understand. There was not talk of "Internet plumbing." None of the new ads mentioned routers.

In 1999, Cisco amped up its marketing efforts with a new brand-awareness program that allowed vendors using Cisco products to put a small "Cisco NetWorks" label on their television, computer, or other device. The strategy had worked for Intel. That company's microprocessors were once every bit as invisible as Cisco's routers. The PC-buying public became aware that there was "Intel inside" their desktop machines only after the company launched one of the most successful brand-name awareness campaigns in history. Intel processors became the standard, and the company's nearest competitors, chiefly AMD, would be forced to market their chips as just-as-good-as-Intel products. Who would have believed ten years ago that PC buyers would become so obsessed with *megahertz* and step so willingly onto Intel's upgrade train? But they did, and many are still aboard. If Intel could do it, so could Cisco.

In 2000, Cisco was anticipating the growth of a consumer-networking market. The idea that everything would soon be connected—from the kids' i Mac to the car's navigation system to the coffeemaker—no longer seemed like science fiction. The nascent consumer market for networking solutions promised, by some estimates, to become a $9-billion-a-year business. It was a market with enormous potential, and Chambers wanted his company to be the name brand in that market, too.

That year, Cisco kicked out an unprecedented $60 million to air its "Are You Ready?" television commercials. "In order to get to the next level, we need the consumer," former Cisco executive vice president, Don Listwin, said in a 2000 interview.[9]

In 2001, the company took a new tack. Building on the success of its "Are You Ready?" campaign, Cisco began running what the company called the "next evolution of the campaign." The tag line this time was "Discover all that's possible on the Internet," and it appeared in television, print, and online. A company press release issued at the time characterized the campaign as a new stage of communications that moves Cisco from evangelizing the Internet to now celebrating how businesses become more successful when the Internet is integrated into their business model.

To date, Chambers has never appeared in a Cisco TV ad, but his face has probably logged nearly as much time on the tube. As his role as company spokesman grew, he found himself talking with Diane Sawyer on ABC's "20/20," sitting down with Charlie Rose on PBS, and talking with Lou Dobbs on CNN so often that they were soon calling each other by their first names.

And yet, the company's product offerings were, and still are, rarely understood. Certainly the general public has only a vague notion of what the company does. Most investors don't know much more. Even in the press, only a handful of reporters really get how the company fits in the technology jigsaw puzzle. For most reports, "networking company Cisco Systems makes the technology that runs the Internet" is good enough.

Not that understanding the difference between a router and a switch really mattered all that much. The ads weren't actually targeted at John Q. Public anyway. Although they would serve the company's aspirations for a presence in the consumer market, one Cisco insider told me that they were really aimed at shareholders, resellers, and partners. The idea was to remind these very interested parties just how pervasive the company's products were. The ads were run during high-profile sporting events, news, and business programming, when corporate decision makers—mostly men—would be watching.

INTERNET ECOSYSTEM

Chambers made it all sound sort of organic when, in 2000, he began talking about an "Internet ecosystem." The open nature of the Net fosters a different kind of relationship among competitors, he said. It encourages complementary business alliances with collaborative, interwoven relationships. It all sounded very friendly, almost collegial, but neighborliness wasn't the purpose of the new model. Chambers was describing a competitive survival strategy that was a direct consequence of the near-universal connectedness wrought by the ever-expanding Information Superhighway.

In a recent interview, Chambers put the concept into historical perspective:

> During the 1980s, companies "did it themselves." The computer industry is a good example: One company would do the components, products, systems integration, consultancy, and applications. That works very well when you're on top in a period of slow change, but it's completely flat in periods of rapid change. During the

> 1990s, the companies that were successful did it themselves and learned how to acquire. In this decade [2000s], the companies that will be successful will also know how to strategically partner in what we call the virtual ecosystem.
>
> This market is just too big and moves too fast, so you need to partner with other companies . . . You've got to learn how to share profits and opportunities.[10]

In the old model, Chambers said, the value chain rewarded exclusivity. But the Internet Economy is, by its very nature, an *inclusive* business environment with low barriers to entry. After all, the Internet is available to anyone, anytime, and at very low or no cost. New ideas and ways of doing things can appear in this open environment from anywhere. It's an environment that simultaneously promotes market participation while encouraging a kind of market anarchy; anyone can get in, and there's no telling what he or she will bring to the party. Here, Chambers said, the old rules simply no longer worked. Here, the market is seen as a web of interrelationships, where knowledge, information, and speed are the new currencies of competition. The company's vision was to create an Internet ecosystem that would eventually connect everyone to everything.

Toward that end, the company created the Cisco New World Ecosystem, which the company bills as a community of technology partners that support open, standards-based architectures and a shared commitment to interoperable, multivendor solutions. Membership is offered to companies that demonstrate leading-edge capabilities and present mutual business opportunities. As of this writing, Cisco and its ecosystem partners were offering a range of solutions for Packet Telephony, Voice Applications, OSS/BSS, Broadband Access, and Solution Integration/Deployment.

Another concept to emerge from this line of thinking was the Internet Quotient, or IQ, which Cisco created to measure how well a company uses the Internet to optimize its internal operations. A company's IQ is determined through a self-assessment test administered over the

Web (www.cisco.com/warp/public/779/ibs/netreadiness/20question.html). Basically, it's an online, yes/no survey that asks questions like "Does the company have successful practices in Internet skills development and knowledge transfer?" "Are sales over the Internet an important component of overall revenues?" and "Does the company have a clearly articulated vision for its market that includes how other companies profit from its success?"

The IQ test also served to quantify a company's potential for participating in an ecosystem-type relationship. Cisco has used it to scope out potential partners of its own. Cisco's own ecosystem includes relationships with companies such as Motorola, Hewlett-Packard, KPMG, and Unisys.

CONSUMER APPEAL

One interesting example of Cisco's Internet ecosystem concept may be seen in the Internet Home Alliance, a nonprofit association formed in October 2000 to bring together companies with an interest in the advancement and promotion of home-networking technology and what Cisco has called the Internet Lifestyle.

Chambers had begun speaking about Cisco's plans to move into the consumer market in 1997. It wasn't long before the company was characterizing the Internet as the "next essential home utility, like gas, water, and electricity." For consumers, this new utility would take the form of a broadband, high-speed, always-on Internet connection that would Internet-enable devices and services.

In 1998, Cisco made a high-profile appearance at the Consumer Electronics Show (CES) in Las Vegas. CES is the industry's largest consumer-oriented electronics trade show, and not Cisco's usual stomping grounds. But Chambers even managed to get on the keynote roster.

Industry observers at the time called the company's move to the consumer side "back-end marketing" because the strategy, if successful, would ultimately drive sales of its high-priced routing and switching equipment. Simply put, the bigger the public network, the better for Cisco. Once high-speed cable or DSL lines found their way to residential users, service providers could offer other network-based services, all facilitated by an advanced network, the guts of which were provided by Cisco.

A year earlier, Cisco had announced a deal with Sony to provide cable modems and associated equipment for the home, based on the emerging standard for the data-over-cable interface specification. That deal was soon followed by partnerships with Microsoft, Intel, and various third-party broadband access providers. Cisco bought a DSL-based start-up called NetSpeed in March 1998, and the company also made a deal with Hitachi to build and market a sub-$500 set-top device capable of offering video-on-demand, voice-over-cable, high-speed Web surfing, and digital cable. And the company's longstanding relationship with AT&T to build a national cable-modem network had a new wrinkle: Cisco was about to be named a key but nonexclusive supplier of cable technology to the telecom giant.

Chambers had always said that his company would end up working with the Sonys of the world.

At CES 1999, Cisco officially announced its strategy for tapping into the consumer market through blazing connections between businesses and the home and the introduction of high-speed "personal networks" within the home. These personal networks would connect individual users to PCs, phones, TVs, and other Internet appliances over a single broadband network.

During his keynote speech, Chambers told conference attendees about Cisco's new role in extending Internet innovation from business to the consumer market, putting his company into a new context. "Eventually all data, voice and video services will be delivered over an open Internet network, changing telecommunications forever," he said. "Like the Industrial Revolution 200 years ago, the Internet will reshape the fortunes of companies, countries and people."

Chambers also announced that his company had formed a Consumer Line of Business group to implement its "personal networks" strategy. Cisco brought in Robba Benjamin, a former vice president at Sprint, to run the new organization.

Cisco threw a lavish coming-out party for its new business group at the CES show. The new consumer group would be pursuing an ingredient-branding strategy, the company announced, but it would not be going directly after the consumer electronics market with any new product offerings. Instead, it would work with service providers to seed high-speed Internet access services for consumers, license Cisco technology for cable and DSL modems to consumer electronics manufacturers, and form partnerships with other consumer electronics and Internet companies.

"The Internet revolution was started by big businesses that understood that the Internet had the power to re-define and re-create the competitive landscape," John Chambers said in a press release issued at the time. "Today, consumers are the driving force in the Internet Revolution. In the Internet Economy, everyone and everything will be connected."

Although Cisco did not roll any consumer products of its own during the show, it did reveal the company's vision of the Networked Home with a model wired with the latest 10-megabits-per-second phone-line connections and a 4-Mbps wireless system for networking PCs with televisions and other home appliances.

The next revolution, Chambers said, would be the connection to the home.

In the summer of 2000, under the auspices of the newly formed Internet Home Alliance, Cisco amped up its efforts to reach the consumer market with another model Networked Home. In an exhibit reminiscent of a World's Fair home-of-the-future display, Cisco built a 1,700-square-foot, fully connected house right on its San Jose corporate campus.

The project was developed by Cisco in conjunction with Digital Interiors, The Great Indoors, Hewlett-Packard, Sears, Roebuck, and Whirlpool—all companies with complementary product offerings that came together in an ecosystem.

The so-called iHome incorporated broadband connectivity via a digital subscriber line (DSL) and a Cisco Internet Home Gateway, Internet-enabled appliances, home-networking products, and services such as an Internet-enabled kitchen. It featured a refrigerator that knew when the door was left ajar and connections that enabled a child to receive homework help from a parent at work or traveling. Lights, music, and security system were controlled with the touch of a button.

The company also announced plans to work with a real-estate developer to build Internet-equipped "smart homes" in a major new residential and commercial community development in West Los Angeles. Every home, office, kiosk, and retail outlet in the planned Playa Vista community would be prewired for broadband Internet access. The company would go on to set up iHomes projects in Australia and Europe.

E-LEARNING

If Chambers has said it once, he's said it a thousand times: "There are two fundamental equalizers in life — the Internet and education." It's another catch phrase, but one that is manifestly near and dear to the CEO's heart. Chambers sees education as a critical means of avoiding a society of technological haves and have-nots, and he sees it as a basic responsibility of the people working in high tech — the people who understand the potential of the technology — to inform the larger society about electronic learning. Cisco defines electronic learning — better known as *e-learning* — on the company website:

"E-learning is the overarching umbrella that encompasses education, information, communication, training, knowledge management, and performance management. It is the Web-enabled system that makes information and knowledge accessible to those who need it, when they need it — anytime, anywhere." (www.cisco.com/warp/public/10/wwtraining/elearning/educate/e-learning_faq.pdf)

For the society at large, e-learning is the great equalizer of the next century. There are no barriers of time, distance, or socioeconomic status when the "educational content" is available on the Internet. The Internet Revolution is giving individuals control of their own lifelong learning. Anyone with Internet access can develop the skills they need to survive and thrive in the Information Age. Cisco considers e-learning to be a horizontal foundation building block that helps cultural and social transformation take place.

That's the pitch, anyway. The jury is still out on exactly how this model will work with established educational institutions. E-learning—also called "distance learning" and sometimes "Web-base training"—has gained some ground in schools and universities in recent years, not as a replacement for traditional classroom experiences or textbooks but as a supplement and enhancement.

Still, its greatest impact has been on business, which has been warming to the concept for years. Initially of interest primarily to technology companies with Net-savvy employees and a burning need for constant skill-set updates, e-learning is making inroads into traditional training markets. The aim is to keep the skills of a company's employees current enough to be competitive in rapidly changing marketplaces. Instructor-led training is expensive and time consuming, and it gets put off. Mergers and acquisitions add to the problem, placing untenable demands on corporate training departments.

When Chambers told attendees at the 1999 Comdex trade show in Las Vegas that e-learning could eclipse e-commerce as a corporate priority in the next few years, he made national news. The *New York Times* picked up his keynote comments the next day, and all at once Chambers was the spokesman for e-learning.

He wasn't the author of the e-learning message, but he has refined the pitch. And he's not the only chief executive who gets this one. One of Chambers's idols, and one of this country's foremost CEOs, General Electric's Jack Welch, has said, "An organization's ability to learn, and translate that learning into action, is the ultimate, competitive advantage."[11]

Chambers has taken up the e-learning banner with even more than his usual enthusiasm, perhaps because of his own childhood struggles with dyslexia. "My parents, who were both doctors, taught me that education was the equalizer in life in the Industrial Revolution," he told *San Jose Mercury News* columnist Dan Gillmor. "In the Internet revolution, it will be access to the Internet and education. Employees who don't have an education level and you don't train aren't going to be able to use the Internet properly, and if we don't dramatically get up the education system in our K–12 level, we're going to be non-competitive as a nation."[12]

Chambers's evangelism of e-learning may have its roots in his personal history—and he certainly has promoted the concept as a societal good—but at bottom it's a business practice, one that its proponents believe leads to greater productivity, increased profitability, and enhanced employee loyalty.

In 1997, the company announced its own entrée into the online training market with a program called the Cisco Networking Academy. At the time it was billed as a new program to teach and certify high-school and college students to design, build, and maintain computer networks capable of supporting national and global organizations. The company later added in-transition workers to its roster of likely students as high-school and college graduates turned to the program to support career changes.

Based on the e-learning model, the Networking Academy delivers educational content, testing, student performance tracking, hands-on labs, and instructor training and support—all online. The program provides industry-standard certification training, and graduates take tests to earn the Cisco Certified Network Associate (CCNA) and Cisco Certified Network Professional (CCNP) certifications.

Company chairman John Morgridge described the academy program as the shop of the twenty-first century. In a press release issued at the time, he said, "It's the first true partnership between schools, government and business since the days of high school 'auto shops.' The difference is, instead of auto mechanics, students learn the conceptual and practical skills necessary to design and manage networks." Morgridge, of course, is another executive who gets it when it comes to e-learning. Education had been a focus of Cisco's chairman ever since he stepped down as CEO in 1995. In fact, he dedicates his time to Cisco's education and government initiatives. "Network-based education and the Internet are the global equalizers in life," he went on to say in the release. "Together they provide the opportunity for governments, businesses, and educational institutions to partner and teach all students regardless of time, distance, or socio-economic standing."

Cisco launched the program with about $18 million worth of equipment and resources, which it contributed to an estimated 57 high schools, colleges, and technical schools in Arizona, California, Florida, Minnesota, Missouri, New York, and North Carolina. In its first year, the program provided more than one thousand students with "school-to-career experience" that they could put to work immediately in the networking industry. As of this writing, Cisco was delivering networking courses via its Networking Academies in 52 countries. The company expected 160,000 students to go through the academy in 2001.

U.S. Senator Jay Rockefeller, who represents John Chambers's home state of West Virginia, lauded the new program. Rockefeller coauthored an amendment to the 1996 Telecommunications Act that linked schools and libraries to the Information Superhighway. "Access to information on the Internet is as important today as electricity and basic phone service have been in the past," he said in a media release. "By equipping our young people with skills they'll need to compete in the next century, Cisco's Networking Academies program is helping to prepare a new generation for a new set of challenges."

Even the U.S. Department of Education applauded the program. Linda Roberts, then director of the Office of Educational Technology, issued the following statement: "The Networking Academies program is in tune with the President's initiatives on educational technology and in the best spirit of public-private partnership. This new program will provide badly needed network support and trained students."

All in all, it was a brilliant move by Chambers and company. Not only would the program provide an industry that was starving for technical talent with much-needed expertise in *their* networking technologies, but the academies would also serve as real-world examples of the

Internet Revolution. The program positioned Cisco perfectly as a key resource for workers and employers in the New Economy.

Not that the company was entirely motivated by self-interest when it came to education issues. Most of Cisco's philanthropic work throughout the company's history has, in fact, been directed at education. Cisco was a founding member of NetDay, a national program to wire America's K–12 schools. It was the first corporation to partner with Internet2, the emerging academics-only network. And the company has supported such educational programs as International Schools CyberFair and the Virtual Schoolhouse Grant Program.

THE CLARION CALL CONTINUES

In April of 2000, *The Economist* wondered about Chambers's basic premise and how it would affect his own company:

> Even if Cisco were to dominate the network as Microsoft controls the PC, it would not enjoy that position for long. If, as Mr. Chambers says, the networked economy is all about speed and continuous change, any firm's dominance will also fade speedily. Cisco could be consumed by the very revolution its own technology has fostered. It may be time to look out for the next start-up that will become the biggest company in the world—faster even than Cisco did.[13]

But Chambers has said that dominance is not, per se, the goal in the New Economy, but rather profits gained through complementary business alliances and collaboration relationships. Sharing profits and opportunities is an important aspect of any alliance strategy. It's not clear exactly how this point of view jibes with Chambers's pronouncements about being the next Microsoft—maybe the guy just can't help being competitive.

Minor inconsistencies aside, Chambers's message has remained on point, even as the fortunes of his and many other companies changed in the summer of 2001. The economic downturn notwithstanding, the networked marketplace still wants companies that can prosper on change, not stability; that are organized around networks, not hierarchies; that are based on interreliant partners, not self-sufficient adversaries; and that are built on technological advantage, not bricks and mortar.

Chambers says that he expects the Internet to become completely pervasive very soon, and although that is a patently self-serving message, he's probably right. And even if he isn't, this first superstar of the internetworking industry continues to sound a persistent, clarion call that can only help his company, whose technology runs through the very heart of the Net.

"We are doing to the Net revolution what mechanical technology did to the Industrial Revolution," Chambers has said. "We are in the right industry at the right time."[14]

NOTES

1. Joshua Cooper Ramo, "Cisco Guards the Gates," *TIME,* June 9, 1997.
2. Andy Serwer, "There's Something About Cisco," *Fortune,* May 2000.
3. Andy Reinhardt, "Meet Cisco's Mr. Internet," *Business Week,* 1999.
4. Eric Nee, "Interview with John Chambers of Cisco Systems, Inc.," *Upside,* July 1, 1996.
5. Ibid.
6. Geoffrey Colvin, "How to Be a Great E-CEO," *Fortune,* May 1999.
7. Ben Heskett, "Cisco's CEO Takes Center Stage," CNET, April 26, 1999.
8. Ibid.
9. Karl Taro Greenfield, "Do You Know Cisco?" *Time,* January 9, 2000.
10. Maurice Geller, "Ten Minutes with John Chambers," *Nasdaq International Magazine,* January 2001.

11. Dermot McGrath, "Will E-Learning Pass Corporate Exam?" *Microtimes Magazine,* April 1, 2000.
12. Dan Gillmor, "John Chambers on Leadership," *San Jose Mercury News,* May 20, 2000.
13. "Cisco Systems: The Dogfood Danger." *The Economist,* April 4, 2000.
14. Karl Taro Greenfield, "The Network Effect," *TIME,* April 10, 2000.

CHAPTER 10

THE STRENGTH OF CONVICTION: WALKING THE TALK

There is an expression used in the tech sector to describe a company that actually utilizes the technology it sells. Such a company is said to "eat its own dogfood." The coarseness of the phrase notwithstanding, nobody eats their own dogfood like Cisco Systems.

One of the things that makes John Chambers such a compelling Evangelist is his company's commitment to using the technology he promotes so zealously. Chambers has been telling fellow executives for years to get their businesses on the Net, and he practices what he preaches. His view is that you have to walk the talk; until a leader truly believes and takes ownership of it and drives it down through his or her company, it doesn't work.

The Cisco facility in San Jose, California (known locally as Cisco City) has been described as the biggest postindustrial park in the world. It comprises forty earth-toned buildings, most of which were built on identical floor plans, and there's a public trolley running right through the corporate campus. Inside, the entire organization—including offices in other locations in the United States and operations in dozens of countries—is connected via an electronic infrastructure that allows Cisco's managers, employees, partners, and customers to share information almost instantly. By uniting employees of the company through a corporate intranet, and connecting them to the rest of the world through the Internet, Cisco has accelerated its business processes and reduced its expenses big time.

Chambers thinks of the Internet as a business medium, and Cisco has utilized it to manage and streamline its internal operations. The company employs Web-based applications to run practically everything throughout the organization, including manufacturing, personnel, finance, and even customer support. According to Chambers, 85 percent of Cisco's orders and more than 80 percent of the company's customer inquiries were transacted over the Web in 2000. He has also said that 70 percent of the résumés the company receives—on the order of 20,000 per month as of early 2001—come in over the Internet.

Chambers believes that this strategy—second only to his obsessive customer focus—gave the company a competitive advantage that allowed it to dominate data networking, and will continue to make Cisco a serious competitor in the new markets it has targeted.

"If you take a look at the point in which Cisco broke away from its competitors in the networking market," Chambers said during his keynote address at the 1997 Comdex trade show, "you can see that it was in 1992. In that year Cisco stopped treating its IS [information services] department as an expense center and started treating it as a strategic advantage."

Using Internet-based applications has allowed Cisco to manage dozens of manufacturing plants as though they were one facility. And it has made the company the undisputed master of the fast close.

What Chambers and company have wrought, they believe, is an Internet culture. At Cisco, everything is on the Web, and the Internet is the answer to everything.

THE ONLINE CONNECTION

Cisco was actually providing online customer support before Chambers became CEO. In April 1992, the company began offering bug information and technical tips through a text interface—no clickable icons. The system was based on e-mail and ftp, and was quite crude by today's standards.

Then in 1996, the company launched its corporate Web site, which it calls the Cisco Connection Online, or CCO. Cisco describes the site as the "foundation of the Cisco Connection suite of interactive, electronic services that provide immediate, open access to Cisco's information, resources, and systems. . . ." Users of the site are called constituents, and they include prospects, customers, partners, suppliers, and employees. According to Cisco, each department within the company runs its own piece of the CCO site. The site has won numerous awards and now has multilingual sections serving over fifty countries.

The CCO Web site is available twenty-four hours a day, seven days a week, and the company says that hundreds of new documents are added to the site every month.

Potential customers access the site to scope out Cisco's products, services, and partner relationships. They can register for seminars, buy promotional merchandise and software, read technical documentation, and download public software files. According to Cisco, nearly a quarter-million prospects log onto the CCO site every month.

The company also uses its Web site as a sales channel. If any of these prospects decide they want to buy something, Cisco is happy to accommodate them via a special section of the site called the Networking Products MarketPlace. The online ordering system enables users to place and manage orders for products and services. According to Cisco, in its first six months of operation, the system processed more than $100 million in orders, and it crossed the $10 billion mark in 1999.

For the folks on the other side of the sales equation, in March 2001, Cisco launched an "e-sales portal," which now serves as a single access point in the CCO for the company's sales force. The Web-based portal integrates and displays real-time data from disparate sources, streamlining much of the grunt work of the sales process. Salespeople can access the site anytime to get timely information about anything from the status of an account to the latest news about a competitor. The site also serves the sales organizations of Cisco's partners.

Current Cisco customers access the company's Web site for technical assistance, software upgrades, and interactive handholding. The company estimates that more than twenty thousand support cases are opened or queried each month, and that more than 90 percent of its software upgrades have been delivered via the Internet. By 2000, more than 70 percent of the nontechnical support queries the company received had shifted from the Cisco's call centers to the Web.

Posting technical-support information on the Internet makes it possible for customers to solve many of their own problems, leaving Cisco's engineers free to focus on the tough cases. And it has saved the company a bundle. Chambers has said that putting customer support online yielded a 200-percent increase in productivity that saved the company nearly $400 million a year. Cisco has estimated that it would have to hire up to ten thousand engineers just for customer support without its online system.

INSTANT BOOKKEEPING

It's August 8, 2000. Cisco Systems' fiscal year ended on July 29, and John Chambers and his CFO, Larry Carter, are presenting year-end results via a live Webcast to analysts and investors from company headquarters in San Jose. The news is good: another 55 percent increase in sales. However, stunning as the numbers are, what is even more remarkable is the fact that the two executives *have* the numbers. Cisco had just closed its books *for the year* through a process known as the "virtual close."

Of all Cisco's vaunted network-supported processes, nothing has gotten as much attention as its ability to provide consolidated financial statements on the first workday following the end of any monthly, quarterly, or annual reporting period. Chambers has described the virtual close as the number-one payback application of the Internet for his company. Reportedly, more than 40 percent of the visits to Cisco Systems by executives for consultations are about the virtual close.

The so-called "fast close" has been around since the early 1990s, when GE and Motorola first began bragging that they could deliver quarterly and yearly financial data to their top executives in a matter of days. Back then, it was a fairly miraculous feat for such large organizations to pull all their numbers together within a week or two of the quarter's end.

Speed here is an undisputed advantage. At one level, it's about being on top of the numbers. On another level, it's about the quality of the information flowing through a company. It was Cisco's CFO, Larry Carter, who took the fast-close concept to the next level.

Carter came to Cisco Systems in 1996. He had spent nineteen years at Motorola, which was one of the first companies in the world to close its books in two days. When he joined Cisco, the firm was growing at a fast pace that would only get faster. Managing the company's internal financial processes had become a struggle exacerbated by the growing number of acquisitions. Back then, year-end closings took fourteen working days, during which the time the company's decision makers were working in the dark.

Carter and the company's finance group were charged with turning on the lights. Specifically, their goal was to establish a system that would allow them to consolidate financial statements in one day, cut finance costs in half, and transform the way the finance group supported the company's decision makers. Toward that end, they developed Internet applications and other mechanisms and put in place a Web-based system for real-time financial reporting, which the company has refined over the years.

Carter wrote about the project in a recently published article in *Forethought,* the magazine of Harvard Business School:

> Achieving the virtual close was not just a matter of rolling out new technology. It required a sustained, company-wide effort to redesign our processes and align disparate parts of our business. Every month, we meticulously reviewed the closing process to pinpoint opportunities for improvement. We established quality standards—and metrics—for all data-collection activities. For example, we standardized the definition of bookings and backlogs, thereby avoiding disputes among sales, manufacturing, and accounting departments about order status. We consolidated responsibilities for accounts payable and purchasing—most finance groups split these tasks—which boosted productivity and cut down on errors. We eliminated practices that yielded little financial gain for the required effort, such as capitalizing assets valued at less than $5,000. Through such steps, we reduced the number of transactions that our systems and employees had to monitor.

Carter is the Tiger Woods of the fast close. He redefined what had been simply—though importantly—a numbers game. Today, it's no longer just about delivering financial statements and balance sheets at the end of a reporting cycle. Now, it's about nonstop monitoring of critical information necessary to run the business effectively. If a Cisco manager wants to analyze revenue and margins based on geography, line of business, product, or sales channel for the day, month, quarter, or year, he or she can do it with a few mouse clicks. While other companies are using maps, Cisco is using a global-positioning satellite.

It took the company eight years to set up the systems that support a virtual close. Chambers believes that most companies could now do it in four years or less. Companies that don't develop virtual close capabilities over the next decade, Chambers has said, will be at a competitive disadvantage.

THE OUTSOURCING CHALLENGE

Not as universally acclaimed as the virtual close, virtual manufacturing, a process that received some harsh criticism in the aftermath of the summer of 2001, makes up Cisco's outsourcing strategy and has played a key role in the company's evolution. Without it, Chambers has said, Cisco simply could not have kept up with the mushrooming demands wrought by the explosive expansion of the Internet.

The vertical integration model is a legacy of the Industrial Age that simply won't work in an Information Age economy. Once upon a time, the big companies did it all themselves. They mined the raw materials, hauled them to factories they owned and maintained, and then sold the finished products through wholly owned distribution networks. But that model has been evaporating in the face of volatile markets that shift and change at warp-speeds.

In their 2001 study of outsourcing, Booze, Allen & Hamilton analysts Bill Lakeman, Darren Boyd, and Ed Frey put the process in an historical context:

> For high-tech supply chains, outsourcing was the panacea of the '90s. Traditional vertically integrated electronics manufacturers, which had been managing products all the way from design and development through manufacturing and distribution, could slash their balance sheets by placing the low-margin operations with hungry contract manufacturers. For companies as varied as Apple, Nortel Networks Inc., and the Nokia Corporation, manufacturing was no longer where they added value; instead, they got paid for understanding customer needs, design, and distribution. Moreover, the speed with which product demand varied stressed their ability to scale up or down in response. As a result, there were tremendous pressures to get these less-profitable manufacturing assets off the balance sheet. . . .
>
> The solution was outsourcing—farm out all those prickly nightmares. Outsourcing was greeted as more than just a strategy; it was

> hailed as a cure-all for whatever ailed the technology sector. The theory was that manufacturing specialists . . . could bring greater focus and expertise to projects, could develop procurement and risk efficiencies better than OEMs, and could lead in innovation if they were encouraged to do so.[1]

Historically, Cisco has been recognized as a company that does outsourcing well. Its ability to meet expanding market demand through relationships with external manufacturers has been all but unrivaled. Cisco doesn't build most of the products it sells. The company owns a handful of plants but maintains relationships with dozens of CEMs (contract equipment manufacturers). An estimated 70 percent of Cisco's orders are received and filled without involving a single Cisco employee. The company claims that outsourcing is saving $700 million a year. And virtual manufacturing allows Cisco to step quickly into new markets. "If we do our job right," Chambers has said, "the customers can't tell the difference between my own plants and my CEMs' in Taiwan and elsewhere."[2]

Critics have charged that outsourcing exposes companies to new and different types of risks, and that's probably true. But it's also true that it may no longer be desirable, or even *possible,* for a high-tech company to own and control every aspect of its business and remain competitive. Outsourcing hasn't proved to be the cure-all everyone had hoped for, but it was the right solution for Cisco, and the company managed its system through delays, shortages, and failing markets better than many of its competitors and maintained a high level of customer commitment.

Cisco isn't touting its virtual manufacturing process in its latest annual report, but the company hasn't stopped outsourcing. In fact, it continues to refine its approach. In early 2001, the company launched a pilot program called eHub, a private, Internet-based supply chain network that links Cisco with its CEMs, its distributors, and its suppliers through a central repository. Among other things, eHub will serve as an advanced warning system. If it works the ways it's supposed to, it will give Cisco a better view of its supply chain, allowing the company to identify and plan for problems before they occur. The idea is to open any clogs in the information pipeline and make the data flowing into Cisco from outside organizations as accurate and timely as the information flowing within the company.

THE EMPLOYEE CONNECTION

The network-based systems at Cisco have made things more convenient for the company's customers, and have enhanced the productivity of Cisco's suppliers and partners—but even if they hadn't done any of that, the company probably would have *had* to turn to some kind of network solution to manage the staggering growth of its workforce. Largely because of its aggressive acquisitions strategy, over the past decade, Cisco has added as many as one thousand new employees in a quarter.

Cisco began migrating its human resources processes to the company's internal corporate network—its *intranet*—in 1994. By 1999, most of Cisco's internal workforce applications had been implemented on a Web site the company calls the Cisco Employee Connection, or CEC.

Cisco describes the CEC as a browser-based workforce optimization command center. Despite the military sound of that description, the Web site is actually more like the company's own Grand Central Station, where employees compare meeting schedules, procure office equipment, request workplace repairs or technical assistance, review their benefits packages, and attend distance-learning classes. They can make travel arrangements through the CEC, submit expense reports, and even order bagels and coffee for an upcoming meeting.

For managers, the CEC provides The Manager's Toolkit, which is a dashboard that displays special links and launches specialized applications. From this dashboard, Cisco managers can call up things like employee salaries and various work records. They can request pay changes, employee transfers, and terminations. They can even write employee evaluations and hand off jobs to other managers when they go on vacation.

Essentially, the CEC has served as a means of off-loading human resources processes to Cisco's employees and managers. This self-service Web site has not only streamlined a number of processes, saving the company a wad, but it also fits perfectly into the notion of employee empowerment that is such an integral part of the Cisco corporate culture. In effect, the CEC gives the company's workforce responsibility for a very high level of self-management.

"Everything is on the Web," a Cisco employee told me. "I mean *everything*. We have access to all kinds of information. The entire employee directory is available to us. We can even see [John Chambers's] information. And we can request supplies and check people's schedules and things like that. It was a little scary at first. It's all there, online, but you have to go and get it. It's what Cisco calls a self-service environment."

E-SCHOOL

One of Chambers's best-known causes is education. As pointed out in Chapter 9, both he and chairman John Morgridge have positioned Cisco as a champion of learning in all its forms, and both are committed to improving education in America. But in particular, Chambers has emerged in recent years as one of the leading proponents of e-learning.

At Cisco, e-learning is another key aspect of the company's self-service, Web-based, empowered-employee culture. According to Tom Kelly, Cisco's vice president of Internet learning solutions, the company utilizes online learning extensively for training, knowledge sharing, and development. In an article posted to Cisco's iQ Magazine Web site, Kelly explained Cisco's view of the process:

> The basic e-learning premise at Cisco is that it's much more than just training—it's a combination of information, education, com-

> munication, and training. We use the same tools whether it's a conference call, a quarterly meeting that Cisco CEO John Chambers does live and pushes out over the network, or a classroom course. E-learning is great for maintaining the company culture, it's great for retaining message clarity, and it gives employees the ability to weave new knowledge into the fabric of their jobs, instead of making it a separate thing.[3]

Unlike traditional instructor-based training, e-learning is available to all of Cisco's employees, worldwide, anywhere, anytime. The company's e-learning programs range from help desk-style knowledge-based systems to just-in-time e-learning and virtual classrooms. Through formal e-learning portals, Cisco provides training in key areas of its business, including manufacturing, worldwide customer service, field sales, company audit, and channel sales. The company utilizes e-learning programs for executive education. And Cisco even makes online training programs available to its customers, partners, and contractors.

Again, the empowerment principle applies. E-learning is, by nature, a self-service process. Cisco enables its employees to learn when, where, and how they want. All the tools are there, but the ball is really in the individual's court.

According to Cisco's latest figures, the company has saved more than $1 billion over the last several years by using Internet-based applications. If it's true, as Chambers has said, that success in business is now driven primarily by a company's ability to leverage the Internet to create intangible value—speed, convenience, customization, personalization, and service—then Cisco will probably be around for a while.

In Cisco's 2001 annual report, Chambers wrote that he believes he is no longer the lone voice in the networking wilderness. The advantages of a networked business are too powerful to ignore, and business and government leaders get it. "I think the vast majority of business and government leaders around the world grasp the potential of the productivity, profitability, and standard of living implications that Internet-based applications offer," he wrote. ". . . leaders truly understand the benefits that these applications can bring, regardless of industry or geographic location."

Even in the wake of dampened growth and big layoffs, executives from other companies still visit Cisco regularly to learn how it's all done.

NOTES

1. Bill Lakeman, Darren Boyd, and Ed Frey, "Why Cisco Fell: Outsourcing and Its Perils," *Strategy+Business,* Q3, 2001.
2. Sandy Chen, "One-On-One With Cisco CEO John Chambers," EBN, April 9, 1999.
3. Sandra Stewart, "Myths and Realities of E-Learning," *iQ Magazine,* September 13, 2001.

CHAPTER 11

GETTING POLITICAL

In 1998, John Chambers journeyed to Washington, D.C., to tell Congress that it ignored the Internet at this country's peril. "My worry is that, if [lawmakers] don't take time to understand the issues . . . they will try to regulate it like it is a company of the old industrial world and that . . . will bring this industry to a halt and allow other countries to move faster," he told *USA Today* at the time.[1]

Chambers was in Washington to address a group of senators and staff during the morning session of the Business Week CEO Summit. He talked with the senators about the impact of the Internet on the global economy, and then he gave a keynote speech at a luncheon sponsored by the Congressional Internet Caucus.

It wasn't Chambers's first visit to the nation's Capitol, and it wouldn't be his last.

The audience for Chambers's views on the Internet, high tech, and the New Economy has grown considerably since he took over at Cisco back in 1995. He has evolved from industry talking head into something approaching a high-tech ambassador. He has the ear of the president, at least in information technology matters, and when Chambers speaks, local and world leaders tend to listen.

Most of Chambers's messages to Congress have been, if not altogether apolitical, driven by practicality rather than ideology. For Chambers, it's all about educating political leaders on the importance of the new Internet-driven economy.

Chambers has, in fact, had the ear of our last two presidents. He was a member of Bill Clinton's Committee for Trade Policy. He has said that Clinton was the first Democratic president to "get it" when it came to the New Economy. Cisco and a number of Silicon Valley companies worked with the Clinton administration to open China's market to U.S. goods, backing efforts to ensure that China would be able to join the World Trade Organization. Chambers also served on George W. Bush's transition team as a member of his Education Committee, and he co-chairs Bush's nine-member advisory council on high technology.

"If there's any group that has its finger on the pulse of the economy, it's the high-tech community," White House Chief Spokesman Ari Fleischer told reporters in 2001. "The President wants to hear their thoughts about the strength of the economy and to share with them his ideas for how to improve it."[2]

Nowadays, Chambers has the ear of many presidents, not to mention a few prime ministers and a chancellor or two. He told the *Washington Post* in 2001 that he talks regularly with every government leader in the world. Hyperbole aside, Chambers talks with many foreign leaders. He has met with Tony Blair in the United Kingdom and John Howard in Australia. He has sat down with Jiang Zemin of China, Chancellor Gerhard Schroeder of Germany, Prime Minister José María Aznar of Spain, and Prime Minister Atal Bihari Vajpayee of India, among many others. He has even shared a stage with UN Secretary-General Kofi Annan.

They all want to talk with Chambers about the New Economy and how they can wire their countries to stay competitive. Chambers has the expertise they need, he has the insight and the vision, and his advice is free. He also has the hardware they'll need, which is not.

But these relationships are more than just business for Chambers. He *likes* hobnobbing with government officials and foreign heads of state. He is an inveterate name dropper in interviews, and his company's Web site features pictures of Chambers with everyone from Kofi Annan to Singapore's Prime Minister Goh Chok Tong. The site features pictures of visits from former U.S. Secretary of State Madeline Albright and Russian Prime Minister Chernomrydin. You'll see snapshots of His Majesty King Abdullah of Jordan's June 2000 visit to Cisco Systems. King Abdullah met privately with Chambers and then joined the CEO and other local tech and government leaders, including San Jose Mayor Ron Gonzales, in a "roundtable discussion" about technology issues.

Heady stuff, but Chambers doesn't seem to have let it effect his ego. Although he made it to Washington for George W. Bush's inauguration, he wasn't at the Republican National Convention. While Bush was accepting his party's presidential nomination, Chambers was fishing.

TECHNET

Journalist and author Michael S. Malone, easily the single most knowledgeable tech reporter alive today—a writer who has been called the "Boswell of Silicon Valley"—noted in an ABC News editorial that many a high-tech exec would probably argue that the worst thing that ever happened to Silicon Valley was that it got noticed by Washington.

A strong strain of antigovernment libertarianism runs through the entrepreneurial culture of the Valley. For many years, the high-tech industry joyfully thumbed its nose at politics. Which is not to say that the region's industry leaders have never run to Washington when they needed help. In the 1980s, when Japanese semiconductor manufacturers began flooding the market with cheap chips, local chip makers obtained tough new trade rules that limited Japanese imports and attempted to force Japan to open its own markets to U.S. competition.

Some industry watchers point to the Microsoft antitrust trial as the wake-up call. Even the tech leaders who were the most vocal critics of the Redmond software maker stopped taking shots at Bill Gates long enough to realize that they could no longer ignore Washington.

Much of the blame for Silicon Valley's political awakening can rightly be laid at the doorstep of one of the Valley's legendary venture capitalists. In 1996, John Doerr, a partner at Kleiner Perkins Caufield & Byers, set out to defeat a local initiative he thought would be bad for business. In the process, he created a political action committee and put the Valley on Washington's radar once and for all. The group he cofounded, the Technology Network—better known as TechNet—is perhaps one of the best examples of the pragmatic nature of Silicon Valley politics.

TechNet is a nonpartisan group based in Palo Alto, California, in the heart of Silicon Valley. Its membership roster includes top executives and senior partners in tech, biotech, and venture-capital firms from inside and outside the Valley. According to the group's public relations, TechNet's mission is "to build bipartisan support for policies that strengthen America's leadership of the New Economy." In other words, TechNet pushes a national technology agenda.

The group grew out of John Doerr's opposition to California's Proposition 211. Drafted by trial lawyers, Proposition 211 would have made it easier to sue companies for poor stock performance. Doerr and local executives (John Chambers among them) believed that its passage would be disastrous for their businesses. What came out of that fight was a level of political proactivity not typical of the high-tech environment.

"[Doerr] has essentially opened the doors to Silicon Valley," U.S. senator Dianne Feinstein said in a 1997 interview. "The Silicon Valley mentality had been, 'Leave us alone. We don't need any help. Just let us do what we want to do.' [John Doerr has] been a voice of reason."[3]

Of course, Doerr can't take the blame—or credit—alone. Chambers was one of the group's cofounders, as was Doerr's fellow Kleiner Perkins venture capitalist Floyd Kvamme and former Netscape CEO Jim Barksdale. Doerr, Chambers, and their brethren make a strange mix of conservative and liberal executives with shared interests in high-tech issues. Consider that John Doerr supported Al Gore in the last presidential election, while Chambers, Barksdale, and Kvamme supported Bush. (Chambers actually gave money to both candidates, but he actively campaigned for George W.)

The group stays focused on tech-friendly issues, such as education reform; broadband deployment; the development of financial accounting standards that will encourage growth, innovation, and the use of intangible assets; and free-market approaches to prescription-drug pricing that will enable investment and innovation in the biotechnology industry. The group also wants a national commitment to research and development, particularly through strong federal funding for the National Science Foundation.

Industry watchers credit the group for pushing Congress to pass a three-year ban on Internet taxes, an increase in the number of highly skilled foreign workers allowed into the country each year on H-1B visas, and securities litigation reform legislation.

TechNet has grown to more than three hundred members nationwide. It contributed $5 million each to Bush and Gore in the last presidential campaign, and raised approximately $130,000 for the campaigns of Democratic senator Joseph Lieberman of Connecticut, Republican senator Orrin Hatch of Utah, and Republican senator John McCain of Arizona, among others.

Steve Case, CEO of AOL Time Warner, is a member. So is Carly Fiorina, CEO of Hewlett-Packard. Marimba CEO Kim Polese, Autodesk CEO Carol Bartz, and former H-P CEO John Young are members, too.

Traditionally, membership in a lobbying group is free, but TechNet charges a minimum of $10,000 for admission to the executive circle. And big companies pay more. And according to a TechNet member, it is understood that members will make donations to some of the politicians they meet through the group.

TechNet courts both major political parties, but insiders estimate that the group has raised more money for the Democrats than the Republicans, so far.

One of the group's main missions is the facilitation of regular face-to-face meetings with government and political leaders. In other words, tech leaders don't have time to go to Washington, but if Washington wants some of the Valley's money, it can find the time to come here. And come here they do. TechNet attracts some of the biggest players in politics to its events. To date, the group has hosted more than two hundred meetings with elected officials and political leaders. Bill Clinton, Al Gore, Senate Majority Leader Trent Lott, and George W. Bush (before he moved into the White House) have all come to Silicon Valley under the auspices of TechNet.

Not that TechNet members don't make their way to the nation's Capitol from time to time. In the fall of 2001, TechNet planned to bestow its Founders Circle Award on two senators and two congressional representatives for their support of the tech and biotech industries at a dinner ceremony in Washington, D.C. About thirty-five high-tech CEOs were set to attend a meeting at the White House and with the House and Senate leadership before the dinner. The event, originally scheduled for September 12, was postponed indefinitely in the wake of terrorist attacks on New York and Washington.

By 2001, TechNet had opened regional centers in Los Angeles, Austin, Boston, and Indianapolis, with plans to open centers in Atlanta, Seattle, and Virginia by sometime in 2002.

GREEN VALLEY

The Internet boom only made things worse—or better, depending on your point of view. Since the mid-1990s, Silicon Valley has been in the crosshairs of political fund-raisers. High tech is the perfect game animal, fat with politically naïve over achievers with only the flimsiest party ties and money to burn.

In the 2000 presidential campaign, Republicans took in $18 million from high tech and the Democrats collected $19.9 million. Chambers was a big contributor to Bush's campaign; he gave George W. about half a million dollars, which is not that surprising. Chambers is politically conservative, a registered Republican. His father once flirted with local Republican politics back in Charleston. During the 2000 campaign, Chambers hosted a Bush fund-raiser at his home in Los Altos Hills, California; it raised $4 million, double the record at that time for a Silicon Valley fund-raiser.

But he also gave around a quarter million to the Gore campaign. He may not be as agnostic about his politics as he is about his technology, but he's savvy enough to invest in the top two candidates. "He felt he had a stake in the winner, whoever it was," a colleague told me. "A Bush White House would be easier to do business with, but it was Gore who really got it as far as the Internet economy was concerned."

Still, it's Bush he likes, personally. Chambers met him several years ago, after hearing business associates in Texas speak enthusiastically about him. The two men had an opportunity to sit down and get to know each other, and they hit it off. Chambers liked Bush's entrepreneurial spirit. He was impressed that Bush had started his own oil-drilling business in the 1970s and put together a group of investors to buy the Texas Rangers baseball club in 1989. Chambers and Bush share similar views on several issues, including the need for open competition among cable, wireless, satellite, and telephone service providers of broadband Internet connections.

DANCING WITH THE MONOPOLY POLICE

"Here's a list of the real no-no's of the antitrust laws, laws that can get our company in hot water." The narrator's voice on the twelve-minute Web-based presentation is deep and somewhat ominous—all the better to scare Cisco's salespeople into avoiding bid-rigging, price-fixing, or collusion with competitors. Steer clear of guerrilla-marketing language such as "kill the competition," "dominate the market," and "own the market," the narrator says. And never forget that "e-mail, notebooks, and hard disks can be looked at by lawyers."

It's a bit of e-learning for the troops, designed to keep them from walking in the footsteps of a certain Redmond, Washington, software maker who didn't tread so lightly. Not that Chambers considers Cisco a monopoly. He's just reminding those in the field that Cisco is a big critter, and the rules are different for big critters. "When you are a cute 30-pound chimpanzee, what people would consider fun or acceptable behavior in your house is not acceptable when you are a couple-of-hundred-pound gorilla," Chambers said in an interview. "To underestimate that would be a mistake."[4]

The Microsoft antitrust trial probably served as a general wake-up call for apolitical Silicon Valley business leaders, but it also served as an object lesson in how *not* to deal with the Feds. Chambers and company were paying attention, and well they should.

Consider one of the consequences of the Microsoft case: The Department of Justice invested heavily in that trial and in the process built a new infrastructure for antitrust investigators, which, at the very least, will make future investigations more efficient. Certainly they'll be cheaper to conduct, and companies will be easier to prosecute.

Cisco's size and market dominance are all but guaranteed to generate antitrust scrutiny à la Microsoft, and the company's aggressive acquisition practices are bound to draw the attention of the Securities and Exchange Commission, but Cisco has managed to keep the monopoly police happy.

It's not just Chambers's considerable charm that has kept Cisco off the watch lists of government regulators. In 1997, the company opened an office in Washington, D.C. to lobby for the usual tech industry issues. The Microsoft antitrust trial put a new issue on the agenda of Cisco's lobbyists.

Daniel Scheinman, Cisco's senior vice president for legal and government affairs, runs the show in Washington. In 2000, he told the *Wall Street Journal* that the Microsoft case added considerable weight to his and Chambers's "belief that we were right to invest resources in Washington."[5]

Rather than dodging the Feds, Scheinman and Cisco executives seek out regulators and keep them in the loop. They approach them very much as they might approach potential customers. They explain their business and their markets to federal decision makers. They develop relationships with them. They even make *presentations.*

Chambers himself reaches out to regulators, telling the Feds, "If I'm ever doing anything wrong, let's just talk about it, and I'll fix it."[6] The strategy has been working so well that the Feds actually seek counsel from Cisco executives on other mergers.

Not that the Feds have left Cisco utterly unprobed. In 1998, the company took a couple of turns around the dance floor with the Federal Trade Commission, after Cisco held partnership discussions with Lucent and Nortel. Nothing came of that investigation. And nothing came of the agency's look in 1999 at a fairly complicated deal in which IBM effectively quit the computer-networking business in exchange for payments from Cisco. In the end, the Feds signed off on the deal.

And there's this: Chambers is not a monopolist by nature. He's the guy who *values* competition. He's the guy who has said, time and time again, that strong competitors make a company stronger.

NETAID

Chambers stepped onto a truly global stage on October 9, 1999, when Cisco Systems introduced one of the CEO's pet projects, NetAid, to the world via the first-ever, intercontinental, Web-based charity concert.

NetAid is a charity-coordinating Web site sponsored by Cisco, the United Nations, and others. It is designed to provide a single access point where people can donate to charitable groups over the Internet. Funds raised through the NetAid Web site are disbursed to antipoverty projects around the world through the NetAid Foundation, which Cisco describes as a "non-profit organization that will be led by an international board of diverse individuals with longstanding commitments to poverty and humanitarian causes."

The NetAid idea is both grand and simple: Use the Internet as a facilitator of charitable giving on a global scale. The NetAid Web site provides a means of making secure donations directly to the UN, and it furthers Chambers's and the company's philanthropic goals. And it is revolutionary, in its way. Nearly two thousand nongovernmental and charitable organizations whose causes fall under its organization's aegis are affiliated with the NetAid site, including Amnesty International, Greenpeace, and Americorps.

The kickoff event was modeled after the July 13, 1985, Live Aid concert, in which a host of rock stars performed for a live television broadcast to raise money for HIV/AIDS research. But the NetAid inaugural did the model one better—two better, actually—with three superstar concerts in three different cities—Giants Stadium in New Jersey, Wembley Stadium in London, and the Palais des Nations in Geneva, with parties and support events held in New York.

In anticipation of a huge response, Cisco pulled out all the stops, technologically. The NetAid site was designed to handle 125,000 simultaneous live streams and one million hits per minute, which is ten times more than other Web sites could handle at the time. Perhaps more importantly, the site could also manage one thousand secure electronic payment transactions per second. (The idea, after all, was to solicit donations.)

Net proceeds from the concerts were flagged for people in extreme poverty in Kosovo and African countries. Cisco underwrote the costs for the NetAid concerts and paid about $12 million for the project's development and marketing. The company also announced that Cisco would be contributing an additional $10 million to the NetAid Foundation.

The company's generosity notwithstanding, it was, at least by a few accounts, Cisco's frugal-but-not-cheap cultural imperative that actually spawned the event. It all started, Cisco insiders say, with the company's decision to attend Telecom, the enormous industry trade show held every four years in Geneva, Switzerland, and sponsored by the International Telecommunications Unit (ITU), a subsidiary of the United Nations. The ITU is a standard body that coordinates global telecom networks and services.

If you're in the telecommunications business, an appearance at Telecom is almost mandatory. But the show is something of a monstrosity. Hundreds of companies show up, and many of them spend in excess of

$10 million to send their people to Switzerland, build a booth, man the show floor, party with the customers, and then tear everything down and come home, all in about ten days. At Cisco, the expense was considered obscene. The show seemed like one big contest to see who could throw away the most money.

But how could a company that was promoting itself as a telecom-equipment provider miss the most important of that industry's trade shows. And although the company might be willing to fly its people to Europe in coach, it couldn't very well scrimp on the booth once its people got there—not if it expected to be taken seriously.

And so Cisco's service provider group was charged with the task of finding a way to make a splash at the show without drowning the company in expenditures. The solution the group came up with was the NetAid concert.

The three shows that comprised NetAid were scheduled for the same day, but each concert started at a different time, due to the different time zones. They all overlapped at 5:15 EDT, in what Cisco called a "moment of unity." At that moment, performers and attendees from all three concerts sang together while watching each other on giant monitors set up at each venue. Sting, Sheryl Crow, Bono, and Wycleaf Jean performed in Giants Stadium. Bryan Ferry and Ladysmith Black Mambazo performed in Geneva. David Bowie and the Eurythmics took the stage in London. And there were more. At the Giants Stadium concert, rockers Bono and Wycleaf Jean performed "New Day," a song they wrote together specifically for NetAid. Michael Douglas made an appearance. Reportedly, Mick Jagger couldn't get into the behind-the-scenes party in New York because no one recognized him. The music drew live crowds of more than 100,000 people. The concerts were broadcast on traditional media. MTV and VH1 carried the shows, as did BBC and TV channels in some 124 countries. And they were broadcast on radio stations in more than 132 countries.

World leaders, including U.S. president Bill Clinton, British prime minister Tony Blair, former South African president Nelson Mandela, Philippine president Joseph Estrada, and South Korean President Kim

Dae Jung were among the first to hit the Web site from their regions of the world.

But it was the *Webcast* that really gave Cisco the bang for its buck. The concerts were videotaped, and PC users could download the Cisco ITTV streaming video software to their machines to watch streaming video of the concerts over the Web. At Telecom, the Cisco booth had seventy monitors showing clips of music, celebrity appearances, and John Chambers sharing a podium with UN secretary general Kofi Annan. It was a first for both men.

Technology journalist Barry Fox called the NetAid event a "great pioneering experiment."[7] The Web site received more than 2.4 million requests for the media stream. Reportedly, the NetAid launch set a record for the largest single-day Internet broadcast event. Cisco equipment and products ran the NetAid concert Webcast, so the company ended up with an amazing Telecom showcase. The rest of the equipment and time was donated.

Cynics might call the NetAid concerts a self-serving public relations gimmick, and it would be hard to argue with them. But the organization still exists, its Web site is still up and running, and NetAid is still working toward its goals long after the conference attendees in Geneva have gone home.

E-DEMOCRACY

Finally, and not surprisingly, Chambers is also very interested in what you might call the procedures of democracy. He worries about voter decline, and he believes that the Internet offers opportunities to reenergize the American electorate. He has suggested that the Internet can reverse the forty-year trend of declining voter turnout, increase access for disabled and elderly voters, and reduce costs and complexity for states and localities.

In his opening address at the 2000 Symposium on the Future of

Internet Voting, co-sponsored by Cisco and the Brookings Institute, Chambers told attendees:

> The Internet waits for no one no country, company or individual. The Internet has redefined traditional business models and is now beginning to reshape the political process. Our country is moving towards an e-democracy in which technology empowers citizens to participate in decisions that shape their future. I believe that the politicians who learn to harness the power of the Internet will emerge as our next generation of leaders.

During his speech, Chambers declared that, by the 2004 presidential election, the "vast majority of states will already have Internet voting." He went on to say:

> But what excites me the most is, it will level the playing field. It will level the playing field where people will be equal in terms of election process. Not held captive by financial systems or special interest groups or the ability on name recognition, but be able to position themselves with a much smaller amount of capital to educate the voter. Much of the same thing has occurred in business. It will simply be, the fast will beat the slow, not necessarily the big will beat the smaller. We have a chance to reengage the American voter in the democracy process, let's lead by example and use this type of exchange of ideas to expand and increase the pace of this process.

Cisco uses its own company Web site to solicit feedback from its employees on key political issues that Chambers and his managers care about, including broadband deployment, education, and what Cisco calls E-Democracy (http://forums.cisco.com/eforum/servlet/Htcom?page=main). The Web site asks:

How can bandwidth ubiquity be accelerated? What are your thoughts on improving the education system and, therefore, the future workforce? If 24-hour, seven-days-a-week availability and convenience, customer focus, and personalization became the norm in the public sector, it would not just make life easier, it would fundamentally change the way that people view government itself. When will this happen?

Soon, if Chambers has anything to say about it.

NOTES

1. Industry Standard, "Media Grok," September 23, 1998.
2. Patrick Ross, "Bush to Host High-Tech Roundtable," CNET News.com, March 27, 2001.
3. Tam Harbert, "Election 2000: A High-tech Watershed," *Electronic Business,* October 1, 2000.
4. Scott Thurm, "Cisco learns from MS mistakes," *Wall Street Journal,* June 4, 2000.
5. Ibid.
6. Ibid.
7. "NetAid sets Webcast record," BBC News, October 10, 1999.

CHAPTER 12

NEVER SAY NEVER

Sometime in the spring of 2000, the dot-com bubble finally popped. The strategy of funding Internet start-ups with feeble business plans and no actual revenues began to seem like a bad idea to the boys out on Sandhill Road, and they turned off the fire-hose flood of venture capital cash aimed at anything with a .com at the end of its name. By the end of the year, more than one hundred dot coms had shut their doors, and more than 200 publicly owned Internet companies were trading at less than 80 percent of their 52-week high.

Soon, the much anticipated e-commerce shakeout blossomed into a real downturn for the entire technology sector. Within a matter of months, an environment that had nurtured some of the fastest-growing companies in history—where employers couldn't find enough qualified people to fill all the job openings—was rife with layoffs and sales on used office equipment.

But through 2000 and into the first calendar quarter of 2001, Cisco seemed to be, if not exactly immune to the effects of the downturn, above the general ruckus of the tech wreck. It was still the fastest growing company in the history of its industry. From 1995 to 2000, Cisco's revenues had grown steadily by an average annual rate of 57 percent, and its market value per employee had more than tripled. In March 2000, Cisco had shot past Microsoft and GE to become the most valuable company on earth. With a market cap of $555 billion, it really was on a trajectory to become the world's first trillion-dollar company. In May 2001, *Fortune* magazine put John Chambers on its cover and wondered whether he might not be the best CEO in the world.

And Cisco was still the company that had, for ages, hit its numbers with a kind of mystical precision. Beginning in October 1997, the company's profits beat analyst expectations by exactly one cent per share every quarter for thirteen consecutive quarters. Cisco execs always knew where the company stood, and the company had truly earned its status as an industry bellwether.

Chambers, of course, remained upbeat even as the economy was turning south. In November 2000, he told *Fortune* magazine that Cisco's biggest problem was managing its accelerating growth. And he couldn't help but put a positive spin on the downturn.

> Yes, the trouble with dotcoms has certainly hurt us, but it has been offset by increases by our enterprise customers . . . We use periods of disruption like this to go after market share. It's very tough to gain market share when everybody's doing great. It's easier when there's a scramble like now . . . [This] reminds me of four years ago, when we were bunched together with Bay, Synoptics, Newbridge, and Fore. Twelve to 18 months later we had broken away. That's what we're looking to do now.[1]

But it wouldn't be long before Cisco found itself tangled in the tech slump along with virtually everybody else—no breaking away from the competition just yet. In February 2001, Chambers announced that Cisco would miss its second-quarter earnings expectations by a penny a share. Beyond the sheer weirdness of the numbers—a penny up for 13 quarters and now down by *a penny?*—the news had a foreboding quality; a scion of the New Economy was faltering, if only a bit. Earnings were down, Chambers said, because of sluggish sales of networking gear to telecom service providers. Sales to other businesses had been slowing, too. Chambers warned analysts that the company's revenue growth for the next two quarters would be flat.

A month later, the news got a lot worse. On March 9, Chambers did something he had sworn to move heaven and earth to avoid, something that would cost him professionally and personally: He announced Cisco's first ever workforce downsizing as a public company. He made the first cut a deep one so that he wouldn't have to slice twice. The company would cut 3,000 to 5,000 regular jobs, or between 7 and 11 percent of its global workforce, and most of its temporary and contract workers, some 2,500 to 3,000 people.

Word of the layoffs leaked on Thursday, but the official announcement was made at the close of trading on Friday, to give the markets a weekend to digest the news. "We're taking these steps because of the continuing slowdown in the US economy and initial signs of a slowdown expanding to other parts of the world," Chambers said at the time. "We also now believe that this slowdown in capital spending could extend beyond two quarters."[2]

And then the worst got worse: In May, Cisco announced its first losses in the history of the company. For the quarter ending April 28, Cisco showed a net loss of $2.69 billion, or $.37 a share on revenues of $4.73 billion. The quarter before, the company reported income of $874 million on sales of $6.75 billion; a year earlier, the company reported $641 million on sales of $4.93 billion.

When the smoke cleared, Cisco shares had lost 80-plus percent of their value. A shareholder who had invested $10,000 in Cisco stock on January 30, 1995—the day before Chambers took over as CEO—would have accumulated nearly $450,000 when the company's stock prices reached their peak of $80.06 per share in March 2000. When the company's stock prices hit $19.05 per share in May 2001, that investment would have been worth a little over $100,000.

Cisco's plans to build a new $1.3 billion headquarters campus in San Jose's southernmost greenbelt, known as Coyote Valley, were scaled back and expansion plans in nearby Fremont were tabled. And along with all the Aeron chairs and IBM Thinkpads from the busted dot coms, Cisco routers began appearing for sale on eBay.

Adding insult to injury, some of Cisco's stockholders sued the company. The $595 million securities fraud lawsuit, filed by a San Diego law firm representing a union pension fund, accused Cisco and its top officers of "inflicting billions of dollars of damage" on individuals, investment funds, and pension funds that purchased Cisco stock. (Cisco has issued 7.3 billion shares of stock, much of which is owned by investment funds.)

Chambers said that the lawsuit was without merit but expected. "It's normal," he said after giving a speech to the Commonwealth Club of California. "I think for the vast majority of companies in my industry, it's just part of doing business."

The news at Cisco was disturbing for investors and employees alike, but the company's layoffs and earnings announcements had wider implications for the high-tech industry at large. This was "Rocketship Cisco," warp-speed pioneer of the New Economy, exemplar of the virtual corporation, and it was *decelerating,* fast. News of Cisco's troubles shattered any remaining illusions that high tech was immune from cyclical economic downturns. And that just plain scared the hell out of a lot of people. If Cisco was stumbling, what did that mean for everybody else? The bloom was definitely off the boom.

100-YEAR FLOOD

Cisco may have been stumbling, but it was hardly out of the race, and in any event, it had a nice, cushy wad of cash to break its fall. How many companies could boast $5.1 billion in cash and liquid securities, $12.2 billion in investments, and no debt? Chambers began shifting the conversation away from issues of a company's market leadership to questions about a company's staying power.

He also continued to evince his characteristic optimism throughout this period. He wasn't a grinning idiot, but he did his best to sound upbeat while managing expectations. In March, shortly after the layoff announcement, he told attendees at a Merrill Lynch telecom conference to remember that even high tech was subject to up and down cycles. He advised them that the recovery from the downturn was unlikely to be V-shaped, but more of a U. It takes time to rebuild confidence in the global economy, he said. He counseled attendees to maintain a long-term perspective on their investments in technology, telecom, and biotech.

"This may be the fastest any industry our size has ever decelerated," he said in speeches and conference appearances. The sudden slowdown was requiring the company to make decisions at "unprecedented speed." In other words, we're doing our best, folks, but we've never been here before.

Despite the climate of uncertainty, Chambers predicted a rebound in global spending that would boost Cisco's fortunes. The company had "long-term expectations for its segment of the IT industry [to] remain at 30 to 50 percent growth per year." Most industry analysts had their doubts about such a rosy prediction, but Chambers was resolute.

And he began wrapping his company's woes in a vivid, and in its way, comforting image—a picture that would earn a *thumbs-up* from the most jaded marketing flack. Cisco and the industry were going through a "100-year flood," he said. Beautiful.

The image made sense, in part at least because Cisco wasn't the only high-tech company that had misjudged the proximity, swiftness, and velocity of the downturn. Nortel lost $2.6 billion in the first quarter of 2001 and announced plans to slash twenty thousand jobs by midyear. Lucent dropped $3.69 billion in its fiscal second quarter that ended in March. And both companies were beating the bushes for new CEOs. By the end of the first quarter, layoff announcements had reached levels not seen since the downsizing epidemic of the late 1980s. And it wasn't just the dot coms; big, established companies were beginning to shovel pink slips.

GROWTH BIAS

But Cisco's problems weren't all the result of outside forces. In the summer of 2000, the company had been working hard to reduce its lead times by stocking up on components. When things slowed down, the company found itself buried in a pile of parts. Shortly after it announced its plans to cut its workforce in March 2001, Cisco revealed that it would to be writing off $2.5 billion in a pretax charge-off for excess inventory.

Clearly, Chambers and company had misjudged demand, but shouldn't Cisco's networked business model have shielded them from sudden market shifts? Wasn't that one of the key selling points of outsourcing, that partnerships with contract-equipment manufacturers kept you from being stuck with warehouses full of unsellable *stuff* when demand disappeared? And anyway, how had they not seen it all coming? These were the masters of the virtual close. They had the power of real-time financial information right at their fingertips.

Critics have argued that it was Cisco's "growth bias" that blinded executives to signals of a pending downturn and drove them to take on so much inventory. Maybe they're right. The company had experienced forty straight quarters of growth—some of it positively meteoric—so a little bias might be inevitable.

Tech journalist and *Radical E* author Glenn Rifkin agrees that Chambers and company displayed a marked expectation that growth would continue, unabated:

> From a distance you can see that there was a belief at Cisco that this growth was going to be intense and forever. Of course, neither one of those things happened. The companies that were buying [Cisco's products] had as much [network] capacity as they needed. And then the bubble burst, so this huge market for dotcom companies that had wanted to buy all this stuff was suddenly gone, and the big companies suddenly stopped their spending, too. The whole telecom sector has gotten killed.

But when Cisco announced the inventory write-off, doubting Thomases everywhere jumped from their chairs and declared the networked business model a failure. Great technology, sophisticated systems, high-quality real-time information—none of it had kept Cisco from taking a hit.

"Do we all really believe that the Internet is dead in the water and that nobody is going to go there?" Glenn Rifkin says. "I think that's an absurd notion. We're in a lull. Lots of CEOs are taking a deep breath. Spending has stopped for a while. People are reevaluating what they've been doing, asking themselves, is this the right direction? That happens periodically in the high tech world. It's not a bad thing."

For Chambers's part, he reminds critics that, although the virtual close is a remarkable tool that lets Cisco look at the financial state of the company on a daily basis, it doesn't allow anybody to predict the future. That's especially true, he says, when it comes to macroeconomic trends, which is how he categorized the rapid slowdown in the overall economy.

PINK SLIPS

In 1999, during his appearance on ABC's "20/20," Chambers told interviewer Diane Sawyer, "I laid off 5,000 people in my last job. We let down our customers. We let down our employees. We let down our shareholders. I'll do anything to avoid that again." But when Sawyer asked him whether his Wang experience had left him depressed, Chambers answered, "I don't get depressed. I deal with life the way it is."

And that's John Chambers in yet another nutshell. The layoffs were tough on him. Insiders say that he barely slept the night before the announcement of Cisco's workforce cuts. He considers it a personal failure. But he did it anyway. He dealt with life the way it was. He had to cut, and so he cut. And he was, by the way, astute enough never to have promised that he wouldn't if circumstances required him to do so. Chances are, though, he promised himself.

According to current and former employees, some of the ideals of

Cisco's corporate culture were seriously tested during this period. Chambers himself seems to have stayed on track with the corporate mores and values he espoused. For one thing, he continued to remain remarkably accessible to his people. An employee who asked to remain anonymous confronted Chambers about the impending layoffs during her birthday breakfast.

"JC was sitting up there with a couple of diet cokes, talking to a couple hundred of us," she recalls. "And he answered every question I asked him about the layoffs. *All* the questions were related to worries about the layoffs. He was incredibly candid. I walked back to my department and asked my manager, why haven't you told us this? And that person's answer was, where did you hear this? I said that I heard it from John Chambers, and it really caused a stir. So, what he was saying and promising had not made it down the chain. And even if it had, not everyone who works in that company does things the Cisco Way."

How the layoffs went depends on whom you talk to, and it varies from place to place within the organization. "The process was supposed to be about figuring out what parts of the company were making money and what parts weren't," an insider told me. "When it came time to figure out who actually lived and who died, the process was more a matter of consolidating your own power base and cover yours and your friends' asses."

"People gave the company the best years of their lives with the understanding that there will be a payout of stock and bonuses down the road," another employee told me. "But all that dried up in the last year. And then they were laid off, had nowhere to turn, nowhere to go. And they were very bitter and angry." Others were less critical and characterized the process as fair and Cisco as forthright.

According to one Cisco employee, although the severity of the downturn that forced the company to cut its workforce was something of a surprise, Chambers and company knew in the middle of December 2000 that something was up. The virtual close process had shown a 10 to 15 percent softening of sales and shipments. "The first one might have been a blip," the employee says, "but when the same softening showed up two weeks in a row, an announcement went out immediately from corporate to freeze all spending, *right now.*"

The company put a freeze on recruitment, too. In the two years prior to the layoff announcement, Cisco had nearly tripled its workforce, adding 30,000 workers worldwide, mostly through acquisitions.

After the holidays, things hadn't improved, and so Cisco's managers were advised to sort out their "five percenters." Many people don't know that Cisco had actually started thinning its ranks before the March layoff announcement, employing a twist on the company's five-percent principle. A current employee explains the concept this way:

> You hire people, thinking that they're right for the job, hoping for a good fit. And you may be right, and you may be wrong, or the job may change. What do you do? You can drag them along, as lots of company's do, or you can give them personal improvement goals, as we do. But at some point, it just makes sense to let them seek opportunities elsewhere. It's an incentive for managers to get rid of their least productive people, because they get to re-hire to get back their head count.

Other tech firms reportedly engage in a similar practice. Sun Microsystems, Nortel, and Intel have been known to ask their managers to grade their employees on a bell curve and then look hard at those at the bottom. The process is known as "ranking and spanking" or the "hell curve."

In January 2001, the word went out to managers to trim their five percenters, but this time around they wouldn't be getting their head counts back. In February, news about the five percenters leaked to a local TV station. When a story that Cisco was laying off 5 percent of its workforce aired on the station's morning news broadcast, Cisco employees clamored for answers from management, and Chambers and company grappled for spin control. This is not a layoff, they said, but our standard operating procedure.

"Of course, it wasn't standard, because they didn't let you replace the head count," an employee told me. "At that point, they also got rid of the contractors. Some got a week notice. Some got a day. Some got a month and a half. It was an easy way to clean house before the 8500."

The official layoffs took place in April. Cisco notified its people over a three-day period. The company provided job transition counseling through Drake, Beam, and Morin, which took over one of the newer buildings on the corporate campus. The company put on a career fair and set up a Web site where the company's partners could post jobs. Downsized employees with stock options that were underwater were allowed to wait up to twelve months to exercise them, compared with the usual thirty to ninety days. The belief at the time was that most people would be placed in new positions within two months. Those estimates were revised as the true depth of the downturn became evident.

Both Chambers and chairman John Morgridge cut their salaries to $1 to save a few jobs. Perhaps it wasn't a great sacrifice for two millionaires, but it was an important gesture. "I don't blame John Chambers personally for this," a laid-off Cisco employee told me. "I think he has our best interests at heart. He's a great human being." Others employees were shocked and outraged at the news. "We couldn't believe it," one laid-off employee recalled. "He said he would never lay anyone off, and he really seemed to mean it. I guess you should never say never."

Cisco tried to soften the blow a bit by offering laid-off employees the option of working at a charitable organization linked to the company. Cisco agreed to pay a third of the employees' salaries, plus health benefits and stock options, if they would commit to work for a nonprofit for a year in what the company calls a "community fellowship." Senior human resources vice president Barbara Beck categorizes these workers as "reduced" employees. Their special status, she says, includes the possibility of being rehired down the road. The idea was particularly appealing to longtime Cisco workers with stocks that were underwater after the downsizing. Groups like the Second Harvest Food Bank; InnVision, a San Jose-based service provider for the homeless; and Catholic Charities of Santa Clara County all welcomed Cisco workers.

Because of these kinds of efforts, many former Cisco employees remained—and remain still—fiercely loyal to John Chambers. But some who were turned out have turned bitter.

Cisco wasn't alone. Intel had revealed its own layoff plans the day before the Cisco announcement. The Silicon Valley-based chipmaker said that it would cut five thousand jobs and warned that revenues for that quarter would be down by 25 percent from the previous quarter. On March 12, Ericsson warned analysts that it would suffer a pretax loss of as much as $513 million in the quarter. The next day, Motorola announced that it would post its first quarterly loss in sixteen years, and that it, too, would be cutting jobs—seven thousand in one of its mobile-phone units. Both Nortel and Lucent had announced plans to cut ten thousand jobs each. Hewlett-Packard announced that it would lay off seventeen hundred, and at 3Com, it was twelve hundred.

None of which Chambers found particularly comforting. "When you do a layoff at a company that has been the most successful in history," he said at the time, "it is traumatic, for everyone involved. Having said this, it's truly a learning experience, and it's exactly what your parents meant when they said it's a learning experience. It's going to last longer than you want, and it's going to be painful."[3]

NAY SAYERS

As Cisco's numbers fell, the business press reacted like a lover spurned. Once the subject of lavish praise, the company was suddenly denounced with snotty commentary and harsh Monday morning quarterbacking. Cisco, "once unassailable, has become unmentionable," said *Fortune* magazine.[4]

"Cisco was the first at the table for a lot of the good things that have happened," says IDC analyst Ken Presti. "When technology got a bloody nose, Cisco was first in line for that, too."

One of the first of the company's strategies to come under fire was the virtual close, but hot on its heels was Cisco's vaunted acquisitions strategy. It had been seen as desperate and imprudent when the press first noticed it, and it was later admired as visionary. Now it was the subject of widespread second guessing. Cisco had focused too many of its resources on acquisitions instead of real R&D. The company had no real research base on which to build during the economic lull. What would Cisco do when economic conditions stalled the acquisitions machine?

But everyone else was in a lull, too, and the critics of Chambers's acquisitions strategy seemed to be ignoring what that strategy had accomplished. Cisco still had a chokehold on networking. It still had customers. It had money in the bank and no debt. Could the company really have aced out the competition the way it had if it *hadn't* acquired companies at such a blistering pace? Without its acquisition strategy, could Cisco really have left its competitors in the dust?

In truth, Chambers's growth-by-acquisition strategy had always been an *innovation*-by-acquisition strategy. He had claimed that 70 percent of Cisco's offerings were developed in-house, but after an eight-year buying spree, industry watchers were grumbling that Cisco hadn't invented anything significant since the router. The acquisition strategy had become a crutch. Cisco's "little D" was spent mostly on cobbling together its acquired technologies. Cisco didn't develop; it *shopped.*

As of this writing, the company had bought only two companies in 2001: Allegro Systems and AuroraNetics—quite a serious downshift from the twenty-three companies Cisco picked up in 2000. It's true that there are fewer start-ups with hot technologies to buy. The venture capital funding was no longer the bottomless well that it used to be, but also, Cisco's shares were no longer the solid-gold coin of the realm they once were. A merger with Cisco was no longer a guarantee of IPO-like riches, and independent-minded entrepreneurs might balk at giving up their independence for Cisco's devalued shares.

But even in the depths of the downturn, in a climate of fear and faultfinding, Chambers would not relinquish his optimism. In a January 2001 interview, he said, "At Cisco we've achieved our company goals, our financial goals, beyond our wildest dreams. I believe we will be the most influential company in history." In August, after all the bad stuff happened, just days before his company would announce a major reorganization, Chambers was as positive as ever. "The strong will get stronger in this downturn," he said.

Call it confidence, hubris, or denial, the guy is no quitter.

And the truth is, here and there, his strategies *did* fail—even Chambers will admit that—but overall they worked well enough to make the once-invisible Internet plumbing supplier into a household name.

NOTES

1. "Tech Is Still The Growth Industry," *Fortune,* November 27, 2000.
2. Rex Crum, "Cisco to Lay Off up to 8,000 Workers," *Upside Today,* March 9, 2001.
3. Jennifer Files, "Cisco Joins Layoff Frenzy," *San Jose Mercury News,* March 11, 2001.
4. Jason Tanz, "The Fortune Hype Index," *Fortune,* June 2001.

EPILOGUE: REORGANIZATION

As the summer of 2001 drew to a close, all eyes were on Cisco. Analysts and investors watched the tech-industry bellwether with baited breath to see what Chambers would do next. He had spent the summer allaying fears, promising a comeback to growth rates of the past, and portraying the downturn as a "100-year flood." And as the dust settled on the tech wreck, he was already looking ahead, to the future of his company, but also to the future of the networking industry.

And although he was doing a lot of talking, Chambers was still listening to his customers. His August announcement of a company reorganization was, he said, a response that was "consistent with customer feedback."

In 1997, the company restructured around three lines of business: large enterprises, commercial customers, and service provider markets. In the new organizational structure, the company's engineering group would focus on eleven key technology segments, including access, aggregation, Internet switching, Ethernet access, network management, core routing, optical, storage, voice, wireless, and the IOS Technologies Division. The company's marketing group, now under the guidance of one leadership team, would turn its full attention to Cisco's corporate message.

The company framed the reorganization as a continuation of its "breakaway strategy" to distance itself from its competitors as an end-to-end provider for the consolidating communications markets. Chambers told reporters that Cisco remained committed to building equipment for telecom networks. "This should not be viewed as a shift in strategy," he said.

The changes would involve no additional layoffs—a claim some of Cisco's rivals could not make. Many were also reorganizing, but some of their plans included additional rounds of layoffs—Lucent was among them.

"Our line of business structure has served us very well in the past, when customer segments and product requirements were very distinct. Today, the differences have blurred between these customer segments, and Cisco is in a unique position to provide the industry's broadest family of products united under a consistent architecture," Chambers said in a press release.

The company also completed its acquisition of AuroraNetics, a San Jose-based maker of equipment for metropolitan fiber-optic networks. The deal was first announced in July. The company's purchasing power had declined with the value of its shares, but Chambers's company was back in the acquisitions game. In October, he announced that he expected Cisco to buy eight to twelve companies in the year ahead, primarily to expand Cisco's fiber-optic offerings. That would be a blistering M&A pace for some companies, but it was seen as a moderate plan for Cisco.

Recent changes in the accounting rules had all but eliminated the financial advantage of using stock for acquisitions, so Cisco's devalued stock was really not much of a disadvantage in the new climate. The company still had lots of money—about $18 billion in cash, liquid securities, and investments. Chambers said that Cisco would be using both cash and stock for future acquisitions. He told reporters that he had waited to make the changes until Cisco's sales had "stabilized" from the rapid declines of the winter and spring quarters.

While Chambers was listening to his customers, Wall Street was listening to Chambers. When they heard him say "sales" and "stabilized" in the same sentence, technology stocks began to show some life. It was all the reassurance investors needed to act. It was what they had been waiting for, some hopeful news about corporate profits from a major market player. Based on August results, Chambers told analysts that he expected Cisco would meet its sales target in its fiscal first quarter, which ended in October. Wall Street liked that news, too.

And along the way, Chambers managed to find yet another weather-disaster metaphor. No flood this time, but instead "tornadoes," or rather, tornado markets. These tornado markets include Internet-based phone systems for businesses, wireless networks for homes and offices, Internet-based systems to streamline the way corporations store data, and gear that reduces Internet-traffic congestion by putting copies of popular digital content on computers in multiple geographic locations.

And Metropolitan fiber-optic networks. This tornado is one that Cisco expects to land Dorothy in Oz. The equipment that connects long-haul networks to local traffic centers could present an enormous opportunity for the company. Cisco believes that it could grow to between $20 billion and $40 billion by 2004.

Chambers's optimism never flagged publicly during the trials and tribulations of 2001. But it was clear to anyone watching him that the spotlight into which he had stepped a few years ago had grown appallingly bright and damned hot. During his appearance on a PBS broadcast of "The CEO Exchange," which aired in September 2001, Chambers told the show's host, Jeff Greenfield, that he missed the good old days, when Cisco was a little-known technology vendor whose products were "bought by IT guys in the bowels of the company." He also told Greenfield about a time when he was sitting at home, watching a basketball game, and heard the announcer say, "That ball fell faster than Cisco's stock."

The line got a big laugh from the audience. It should have. It was a good line; a bit personal, a bit self-deprecating, but on point, underscoring the company's notoriety and status. There was no doubt about it: Chambers had the company spokesperson thing down. This was every bit the man of whom Salomon Smith Barney analyst Peter Swartz once said, "Chambers is a West Virginia choirboy, soft-spoken, articulate, but inside he'll eat you up."

It's fair to say that the verdict is still out on John Chambers the

CEO. His achievements in business are legendary. His failures, mythic. His optimism, unassailable. The setbacks he experienced during the economic downturn served only to make him even more resolutely positive and more determined to win. And maybe a little wiser.

Whether Chambers will successfully meet the coming challenge of managing his company in a down economy remains to be seen. What he does next may well be his true test as a CEO, and his legacy.

Appendix A

CISCO'S ACQUISITIONS HISTORY

September 21, 1993—Crescendo Communications

July 12, 1994—Newport Systems Solutions: software-based routers for remote network sites.

October 24, 1994—Kalpana, Inc.: modular and stackable platforms that extend the usability and data capacity of existing Ethernet LANs.

December 8, 1994—LightStream Corporation: enterprise ATM switching, workgroup ATM switching, LAN switching, and routing.

August 10, 1995—Combinet, Inc.: maker of ISDN (Integrated Services Digital Network) remote-access networking products. Cisco's integration of Combinet broadens the solutions Cisco offers for telecommuting and strengthens its expertise in ISDN technology.

September 6, 1995—Internet Junction, Inc.: developer of Internet gateway software connecting desktop users with the Internet. Internet Junction products provide users with Internet gateway software for central and remote office Internet access.

September 27, 1995—Grand Junction Networks, Inc.: inventor and leading supplier of Fast Ethernet and Ethernet desktop switching products.

October 27, 1995—Network Translation, Inc.: manufacturer of cost-effective, low-maintenance network address translation and Internet firewall hardware and software.

January 23, 1996—TGV Software, Inc.: supplier of Internet software products for connecting disparate computer systems over local area, enterprise-wise, and global-computing networks. Extended Cisco's software product line to include network applications and services used to build corporate intranets.

April 22, 1996—StrataCom, Inc.: leading supplier of ATM and frame relay high-speed wide area network (WAN) switching equipment that integrates and transports voice, data, and video. Allowed for end-to-end solutions.

July 22, 1996—Telebit Corp.: modem ISDN channel aggregation (MICA) technologies. High-density digital modem technology.

August 6, 1996—Nashoba Networks, Inc.: token ring switching technologies. Token Ring LAN switching products, to be targeted at workgroup and backbone environments.

September 3, 1996—Granite Systems Inc.: standards-based multiplayer gigabit Ethernet switching technologies.

October 14, 1996—Netsys Technologies, Inc.: network infrastructure management and performance analysis software.

December 1996—Metaplex, Inc.: network product development in the IBM enterprise marketplace. Allows customers to easily migrate from SNA to IP.

March 27, 1997—Telesend: WAN products. Through acquisition, Cisco announced a new channel unit for D4 DSL Frame Muxes, the Cisco 90i, which provides telecommunications carriers with a more cost-effective way to deliver high-speed data services for Internet and intranet access applications.

June 9, 1997—SkyStone Systems Corp.: high-speed SONET/SDH technology. At the time, this was the emerging transport technology used for carrying info in very high-capacity backbone networks, such as those operated by telecom carriers and large ISPs.

June 24, 1997—Global Internet Software Group: Centri Security Manager Windows NT firewall. Turnkey solution for small and medium businesses.

June 24, 1997—Ardent Communications Corp.: communications support for compressed voice, LAN, data and video traffic across public and private frame relay and ATM networks. Integration of voice, video, and data.

July 28, 1997—Dagaz (Integrated Network Corporation): suite of products for high-speed information transmission over existing copper phone lines.

December 22, 1997—LightSpeed International, Inc.: voice protocol conversion and intelligent call control software, enabling signaling to be transmitted among diverse sets of voice protocols and applications. Technology allows different phone and communications systems to work together in a seamless fashion.

February 18, 1998—WheelGroup Corp.: end-to-end security solutions. Intrusion detection and security scanning software products. Scanning technology identifies network security gaps—this new class of detection and scanning technology to be referred to by Cisco as "active audit."

March 11, 1998—NetSpeed, Inc.: added customer premise equipment, central office products and broadband remote access to Cisco's DSL product portfolio. DSL products deployed in carrier networks, like Cincinnati Bell, US West, etc. Complemented the Dagaz acquisition of 1997.

March 11, 1998—Precept Software, Inc.: multimedia networking software company. Complements Cisco's strategy of developing networking solutions that integrate voice, data, and video traffic. Precept's IP/TV product sends live or prerecorded digital video and audio to large numbers of users over any IP-based local or wide area network.

May 4, 1998—CLASS Data Systems: products that allow control capabilities so that network managers can allocate network resources according to company priorities.

July 28, 1998—Summa Four, Inc.: programmable switches that allow for telephony applications to new and existing service providers, and expands those services to voice-over IP infrastructure.

August 21, 1998—American Internet Corporation: software for IP address management and Internet access.

September 15, 1998—Clarity Wireless Corporation: wireless communication technology for computer networking and Internet service markets. Complements Cisco's last-mile solutions, including dial, xDSL, and cable.

October 14, 1998—Selsius Systems, Inc.: supplier of network PBX systems for high-quality telephony over IP networks. Data/voice integration.

December 2, 1998—Pipelinks, Inc.: SONET/SDH routers capable of transporting circuit-based traffic and routing IP traffic simultaneously. Using Cisco's IOS software to compliment the Pipelinks products, service providers can offer new services such as managed Internet access and native LAN services over an existing TDM infrastructure.

April 8, 1999—Fibex Systems: integrated access digital loop carrier (IADLC) products that combine traditional voice services with data services using ATM as the underlying architecture. Helps service providers transition voice/data traffic to cell/packet networks while maintaining traditional phone business using existing circuit infrastructure.

April 8, 1999—Sentient Networks, Inc.: industry's highest density ATM circuit emulation services (CES) Gateway, capable of transporting circuit-based private line services across packet-based ATM networks. Will help service providers to migrate to cell and packet-based networks.

April 13, 1999—GeoTel Communications Corp.: software that integrates enterprise data applications with voice infrastructure devices such as PBXs to deliver integrated data and voice to call centers over an Intranet infrastructure and the PSTN. Furthers Cisco strategy to create an open data and voice software infrastructure.

April 28, 1999—Amteva Technologies, Inc.: IP-based unified communications middleware that consolidates voicemail, e-mail, and fax on a single IP network, accessible independent of location, time, or device. Unified communication.

June 17, 1999—TransMedia Communications, Inc.: technology that unites multiple networks (ATM, IP, PSTN) of public voice communications, providing successful transition to New World networks.

June 29, 1999—StratumOne: semiconductor products for very high-speed wide area databased interfaces.

August 16, 1999—Calista, Inc.: technology that allows legacy digital phones to interoperate with New World voice-enabled switches and routers in a feature transparent fashion. Allows products from different manufacturers to interoperate and thereby allows customers to preserve their investments in existing digital phones and wiring.

August 18, 1999—MaxComm Technologies, Inc.: enables the delivery of additional voice lines and high-speed data over broadband to the home. Utilizes existing wiring, customer installable, allows more phone lines per wire pair. Delivers increased features to the home with minimal deployment costs.

August 26, 1999—Monterey Networks, Inc.: optical transport networks. Helps service providers handle rapid growth of Internet traffic.

August 26, 1999—Cerent Corporation: optical transport market, a market forecasted to grow to $17BB by 2002. SONET ADM equipment that's a fundamental building block in voice and data networks and is used to add and remove lower-speed traffic from higher-speed optical rings.

September 14, 1999—Cocom A/S: standards-based solutions over cable TV networks. Digital video broadcasting and digital audio and video council-based head end and cable modem solutions that connect homes and businesses to the Internet and to interactive services at high speeds. Will enhance Cisco's cable solutions.

September 22, 1999—WebLine Communications Corp.: Customer-interaction management software for Internet customer service and e-commerce.

October 26, 1999—Tasmania Network Systems, Inc.: network-caching software technology. Content-networking services, including content-aware network caching that accelerates content delivery and overall network performance by localizing traffic patterns.

November 9, 1999—Aironet Wireless Communications, Inc.: Standards-based high-speed wireless LAN products that enable PC users to establish and maintain wireless network connections.

November 11, 1999—V-Bits, Inc.: standards-based digital video-processing systems for cable television service providers. Enhances Cisco's solution for streamlined broadband networks supporting data, voice, and video services.

December 16, 1999—Worldwide Data Systems, Inc.: consulting and engineering services for converged data and voice networks. Enhances Cisco's solution for accelerating deployment of data, voice, and video networks for enterprise and service provider customers.

December 17, 1999—Internet Engineering Group, LLC: high-performance software. Strengthens Cisco's optical-internetworking strategy.

December 20, 1999—Pirelli Optical Systems: dense wave division multiplexing (DWDM) equipment. Optical transport systems.

January 19, 2000—Compatible Systems Corp.: standards-based VPN solutions for service provider networks. IPSec architectures for VPN services.

January 19, 2000—Altiga Networks: integrated VPN solutions for remote access applications. Complements Cisco's family of VPN routers and security appliances.

February 16, 2000—Growth Networks, Inc.: Internet switching fabrics, new category of networking silicon. Their technology allows service providers to deploy advanced systems with switching capacities that scale from 10s of gigabits per second (Gbps) to 10s of terabits per second (Tbps).

March 1, 2000—Atlantech Technologies Ltd.: network element management software that configures and monitors network hardware.

March 16, 2000—JetCell, Inc.: standards-based, in-building wireless telephony for corporate networks.

March 16, 2000—infoGear Technology Corp.: Internet appliances and software to manage those appliances for Internet access.

March 29, 2000—SightPath, Inc.: appliances for creating intelligent content delivery networks (CDNs). Will allow Cisco customers to create CDNs using existing Internet and intranet infrastructure.

March 2000—Cisco's market cap hits $555BB, making it the world's most valuable company.

April 11, 2000—PentaCom Ltd.: products implement spatial reuse protocol (SRP), which allows IP-based metropolitan networks to offer protection and restoration benefits equal to SONET-based networks while doubling bandwidth efficiency. Underscores Cisco's strategy to deliver end-to-end IP-based solutions for service providers to deploy advanced data, voice, and video services.

April 12, 2000—Seagull Semiconductor, Ltd.: develops silicon technology. Cisco acquired Seagull subsidiary that is comprised of Seagull's core technology development team. High-speed silicon expertise that will allow Cisco to accelerate the development of terabit performance routers (complimentary to Growth Networks acquisition in February 2000).

May 5, 2000—ArrowPoint Communications, Inc.: provider of content switches that optimize delivery of Web content. Products will enable ISPs, Web-hosting companies, and other Cisco customers to create a faster, more reliable Web experience and will allow their services to direct traffic based on information such as the content being requested and the frequency of the content request.

May 12, 2000—Qeyton Systems: develops metropolitan dense wave division multiplexing (MDWDM) technology. Expands Cisco's optical-networking capabilities. DWDM technology links carriers points of presence (POPs) and customer sites with an optical ring and enables increased capacity without the need to add or lease new fiber in the metropolitan areas.

June 5, 2000—HyNEX, Ltd. (subsidiary of Elbit, Ltd., Nasdaq-listed company at ELBTF): intelligent access devices for ATM network providers. Accelerates deployment of IP+ATM networks in international markets.

July 7, 2000—Netiverse, Ltd.: content acceleration technology that enhances the performance and functionality of networking devices. Helps customers to distribute Web content and manage large amounts of Internet traffic. Technology can be used across multiple product lines and will be integrated into Cisco's existing content-networking solutions.

July 25, 2000—Komodo Technology, Inc.: voice-over IP (VoIP) devices that allow analog telephones to place calls over IP-based networks. Service providers can support IP telephone customers who have analog telephones, which can be connected directly to Komodo's product.

July 27, 2000—NuSpeed Internet Systems, Inc.: technology that connects storage area networks and IP networks. Technology will be used by Cisco to interconnect storage area networks with MANs, WANs, and LANs.

August 1, 2000—Ipmobile, Inc.: software that enables service providers to build IP-based wireless infrastructures known as third-generation, or "3G," networks to allow the creation of a mobile wireless Internet (convergence of Internet-related data services and mobile wireless services).

August 31, 2000—PixStream, Inc.: hardware and software that allows for the distribution and management of digital video and streaming media across broadband networks. Their senior management and engineering staffs have a lot of video-networking expertise.

September 28, 2000—IPCell Technologies, Inc.: software for broadband access networks combining IP and telephony services. Interface between call control and service layers for voice-over packet applications.

September 28, 2000—Vovida Networks, Inc.: communications software and supplier of networking protocols. VOCAL (Vovida Open Communication Application Library)—open-source packet telephony networking software that allows developers to use code royalty-free while benefiting from improvements contributed by the global development community.

October 20, 2000—CAIS Software Solutions: software to provide and manage high-speed, broadband Internet services in the multi-unit building market. Enables broadband service providers to deploy, market, and operate services for the multifamily, multitenant, and hospitality markets.

November 10, 2000—Active Voice Corporation: IP-based unified messaging for enterprise and small/medium business customers. Consolidates voice mail, e-mail, and fax messages on a single IP network, accessible independent of location, time, or device. Important initiative for Cisco. Key to their architecture for voice, video, and integrated data (AVVID) for corporate enterprise.

November 13, 2000—Radiata, Inc.: chipsets for high-speed wireless networks. Faster data rates for next-generation wireless networks.

December 14, 2000—ExiO Communications, Inc.: in-building, wireless technologies for corporate networks based on standard, code division multiple access (CDMA) technologies.

July 11, 2001—AuroraNetics, Inc.: developer of 10 Gbps silicon technology for metropolitan fiber networks. This silicon technology is used in data-optimized fiber rings known as resilient packet rings (RPR), which offer the ability to create high-speed metropolitan networks that efficiently transport significant amounts of IP and other data, including Ethernet. Will license this silicon design to companies interested in producing and participating in the development of 10 Gbps SRP RPR-based solutions. This will help accelerate industry availability of 10 Gbps RPR products.

July 27, 2001—Allegro Systems, Inc.: developer of VPN acceleration technologies to enhance performance and functionality of secure networking platforms. This technology complements Cisco's existing portfolio of security products.

INDEX

D

E

M

N